Prais

In *Strangers in Paradise*, Jim ~~~~~~~~~~~ with his readers the challenges that any immigrant faces in adjusting to new surroundings. However, these immigrants are the newly affluent, striving to make a successful transition to their new land of wealth. His book provides a unique perspective in understanding these wealth issues and offers excellent strategies for ensuring success in this journey. This book is an invaluable resource to advisors in the wealth management field, as well as those on the journey.

> Lee Hausner, Ph.D., Senior Managing Director, First Foundation Advisors, and author of *Children of Paradise: Successful Parenting in Prosperous Families* and *The Legacy Family: The Definitive Guide to Creating a Successful Multigenerational Family*

In his new book, Jim Grubman offers us something truly unique about wealth: a framework that family advisors or family members can use to answer one question—why? Why do some families fare better than others, and why is one approach likely to be more successful than another? Jim helps answer these questions. In the process, he provides tools to predict and prepare for the bumps in the road that families are likely to encounter. His innovative use of research around cultural immigration and adaptation illuminates the paths of successful families unlike anything I have read before. I highly recommend this book!

> J. Richard Joyner, President and CEO, Private Wealth Management, Tolleson Wealth Management

Strangers in Paradise opens a fresh dialogue for those in a family who create wealth and those who receive it. One side speaks to the belongingness in new surroundings of the "Immigrants" from the middle class who create the wealth, with their nostalgia for values that were and awareness—even embarrassment—about the very different values of the recipients of their wealth. The other side brings forward those very different values and perspectives adopted by the "Natives" of these surroundings, for whom such wealth may be generations old. Dr. Grubman offers a family in this situation a safe means to have this discussion and to explore its ramifications. It is an enormous gift.

> James E. Hughes, Jr., author of *Family Wealth: Keeping It in the Family* and co-author of *The Cycle of the Gift: Family Wealth and Wisdom.*

Sometimes, in truly significant discussions, there comes a "eureka" moment when the pieces suddenly click into place and we see things in a whole new way. For families of wealth and their advisors, this book *is* that moment. With brilliance and clarity, Dr. Grubman maps out a new direction that redefines the challenge of adapting to significant wealth. He hand-delivers to wealthy families a vision of their sustainable future.

Suzanne Slater, Family Wealth Consultant, Gifted Generations

Strangers in Paradise captures what it feels like to be "in the shoes" of wealth's creators or inheritors. It is a must-read for parents who want to understand their children, children who want to understand their parents, and anyone with wealth seeking to understand themselves.

Keith Whitaker, Ph.D., Principal, Wise Counsel Research Associates, and co-author of *The Cycle of the Gift: Family Wealth and Wisdom*

The explanatory power of the Immigrant and Native metaphor offers a framework for understanding very complex circumstances. After finishing *Strangers in Paradise*, readers will say: "Now I get it!" And, importantly, they will recognize the steps necessary to thrive in The Land of Wealth.

Hartley Goldstone, J.D., M.B.A., co-author of *TrustWorthy: New Angles on Trusts from Beneficiaries and Trustees.*

Strangers in Paradise builds nicely on Jim Grubman's work with Dennis Jaffe to clarify life with wealth. The book is a nuanced, intelligent exposition that spares us the platitudes of many advisory texts. It outlines the complexity faced by individuals and families when financial wealth is either present from the start or arrives along the way. Beyond being descriptive, this work also brings fresh ideas on how to process the transitions of wealth in support of well-being and integration of identity. It is written in a style accessible to families and their advisors - and they both really need to read this. The framework presented and the substantial use of cases are going to resonate well with virtually any reader inhabiting or advising in the culture of wealth.

G. Scott Budge, Ph.D., Managing Director, RayLign Advisory LLC, and author of *The New Financial Advisor: Strategies for Successful Family Wealth Management*

Becoming wealthy is central to the American Dream. However, when the Dream is achieved, then what? *Strangers in Paradise* carefully addresses how to live with wealth in a constructive manner, now and for generations to come. Applying insights from research and face-to-face work with the wealthy and their advisors, Dr. Grubman has discovered and applied his unique approach with great success. Whether you are a wealth holder, family member or an advisor to the wealthy, this book is an indispensable guide.

Gary Shunk, CEO, Family Wealth Dynamics

Strangers in Paradise

Strangers in Paradise

HOW FAMILIES ADAPT TO WEALTH
ACROSS GENERATIONS

—

James Grubman, Ph.D.

Printed in the United States of America

Grubman, James.
Strangers in Paradise: How Families Adapt to Wealth Across Generations / James Grubman.

ISBN-13: 978-06-15894355 (FamilyWealth Consulting)
ISBN-10: 0615894356

Book design: VJB/Scribe
Cover art: Michael Gibbs

To my wonderful family
In my heart, always

———

Contents

Foreword
by Dennis T. Jaffe, Ph.D.

I AM PLEASED TO INTRODUCE A UNIQUE APPROACH TO THE DYNAMics of family wealth, written by my longstanding friend, colleague, and collaborator, Dr. James Grubman.

Strangers in Paradise does not fit within any of the standard genres of financial books. It doesn't offer tips and tools on how to join the ranks of the wealthy. It doesn't share commonsense "secrets" of entrepreneurs on becoming successful, nor does it regale the reader with lurid details about the rich and famous. It isn't a rehashing of standard ideas about the issues facing financially prosperous families. Rather, it illuminates exciting new insights into the nature of wealth in families, vividly defining the *predictable* challenges that arise between the wealth-acquiring generation and their offspring who grow up in affluent surroundings.

Strangers in Paradise maps the influence of wealth as it enters a family and flows across generations. This book is a guide through the difficult terrain that too often leads to the dissipation of family wealth. Jim's lesson is that a family, able to understand and *anticipate* the difficulties resulting from acquiring wealth, can better face the unwelcome pressures they encounter when trying to enjoy the fruits of their labor.

The Origins of a New Approach

The wisdom within these pages has been developing for a long time, from multiple directions. One origin derives from the early 1980s when the study of wealth arose within the cross-disciplinary field of family business. The complicated nature of families in business began to focus on matters such as family conflict, work roles, inheritance, and the many connections of money to power, love, respect, and family justice.

Another source was added in the 1990s with the evolution of the field of financial planning and advising. Financial advisors began to look beyond the technical aspects of wealth preservation toward the values, behaviors, desires, and legacies that successful families wanted to pass on to their children. Through what became known as the areas of life planning and family dynamics, families were encouraged to hold conversations to make decisions together and to consciously pass along values and legacy in relation to work and money for their children.

A third source came from developments in the professional field of psychological counseling. While wealth has always been known to have a deep impact on the emotional life of the family, the topic seldom comes up in therapy to any effective degree. In our respective backgrounds as psychologists, Jim and I each experienced how many of our newly wealthy clients felt that talking about an abundance of money was taboo. Yet we heard fears from parents about the strains of giving money to their children, and from their children about how confusing, stingy, or controlling their parents behaved regarding money. Wealthy parents frequently have contradictory feelings about raising their children in a privileged environment. Parents are proud of what they can offer their children, but they also simultaneously live in fear that their children will be corrupted by the family's affluence. Yet wealth creators and their families can't easily find guidance and support for something they expected would be easy. Over the past twenty years, the field of wealth counseling emerged to deal with these and many other issues. Wealth counselors began to develop new understanding and approaches for helping prosperous families cope with these natural stresses.

A Spark of Insight: "Immigrants and Natives"

While these professional currents were converging, Jim and I were traveling along intersecting paths in our work as consultants in wealth psychology. During the early part of the new millennium, we separately created surprisingly similar graduate level courses on what we called "The Psychology of Wealth." To our knowledge, these were the only two courses of this type at the time. We were introduced and began to share ideas.

Our first collaboration resulted in the publication of a 2007 article on the psychology of wealth in the *Journal of Wealth Management*. This review article delved deeply into the contrasting challenges experienced by the old and new generations in a wealthy family, what we called "the Acquirers' and Inheritors' Dilemmas." During the writing of that article we were blessed with the spark of insight that has led directly to the book you now are reading.

We began to feel that, while individual personalities are important influences on family behavior, many family dynamics in wealth are not the result of personality differences. We identified universal patterns in families. Some of the difficulties in sustaining family wealth seemed to arise because wealth acquirers grew up in an economic culture that was poor or middle class. After they acquired wealth, they often did not know how to act or what to do. As we put it, they acted like *immigrants* to a new "Land of the Wealth," raising children and grandchildren who are *native* to that land. The elders came from scarcity while their children lived in abundance. These cultural differences led the different generations to different ways of seeing work, risk, opportunity, and life goals.

Predictable Challenges along a Difficult Journey

The outcome is a book-length exploration by Jim of the "Immigrants and Natives" metaphor, benefiting from the literature and teachings of cross-cultural psychology and sociology. *Strangers in Paradise* explores the challenges that emerge when wealth acquirers move from a culture of limited means into a world where opportunities, choices, and resources can seem limitless. The children of wealth acquirers grow up in this new realm, where the survival skills and values of their parents may seem irrelevant to their experiences and needs. These basic differences in life experience give rise to challenges in parenting, family cohesion, identity, and harmony.

Jim and I share the view that these challenges are neither pathological nor unavoidable. They are the predictable consequences of the journey of successful families from their roots in middle- or working-class life, through their entry into the world of great wealth, to the desire to productively pass on wealth to their children and later generations.

Jim proposes that those new to wealth must teach their children two broad sets of skills. First, parents need to prepare their children to become independent, self-sufficient, and purposeful in their individual path in life. Second, and no less important, wealth inheritors must learn to work together to manage their shared family assets, collaboratively. The second and third generations must learn to work as a team, setting individual and shared goals, making compromises, and helping each other along their intertwined paths.

By illuminating the nature of the different worlds of acquirers and inheritors, *Strangers in Paradise* helps a family prepare for this generational shift. The book offers a roadmap for the family to integrate new wealth and use it wisely to further their shared dreams, values, and aspirations.

I am honored to work with Jim and to benefit from his wisdom and insight. I believe his book is a rich treasure for parents and advisors. Read on. Your life and work in relation to family wealth will never be the same.

DENNIS T. JAFFE Ph.D. is professor of organizational systems and psychology at Saybrook University in San Francisco, and an advisor to families about family business, governance, wealth, and philanthropy. He is author of *Stewardship in Your Family Enterprise: Developing Responsible Family Leadership Across Generations; Working with the Ones You Love: Building a Successful Family Business;* and, *Working with Family Businesses: A Guide for Professional Advisors;* as well as the management books *Rekindling Commitment, Getting Your Organization to Change,* and *Take this Work and Love It,* as well as more than a hundred management and psychology articles. In 2005 he was awarded the Richard Beckhard Award for service to the field from the Family Firm Institute. He received his B.A. degree in philosophy, M.A. in management, and Ph.D. in sociology, all from Yale University, and is a licensed psychologist.

Acknowledgments

IT HAS TAKEN MORE THAN THREE YEARS FOR THIS BOOK TO SEE THE light of day. I want to acknowledge the many cherished people who helped make it happen.

First, I want to express my deep appreciation to—and for—my long-time colleague and collaborator, Dr. Dennis Jaffe. For a decade now, Dennis has been a source of wisdom, a sounding board, a strong supporter, a fellow pioneer, and a warm-hearted friend. Co-creating so many wonderful ideas and directions with Dennis has been the highlight of my professional life in wealth counseling. I especially want to thank him for his generosity and selflessness in encouraging me to pursue my curiosity about the underpinnings of our unique metaphor of "Immigrants and Natives."

I also want to thank a few colleagues who were particularly instrumental in nurturing me and the book along the way. Lee Hausner launched me on this project when she offered to be my coach to get it done. She then called, emailed, cajoled, listened, pushed, praised, and advised me as the best coaches do. Without her injecting momentum at various points, this book would still be languishing as a "to-do" project. Suzanne Slater, Keith Whitaker, Scott Budge, Jay Hughes, Hartley Goldstone, John A. Warnick, Richard Joyner, Roy Ballentine, Gary Shunk, Jamie Traeger-Muney, Cheryl Holland, Susan Colpitts, and many other esteemed professionals provided thoughtful insights at important stages, for which I am grateful.

The concepts and experiences outlined in this book were borne out of my work over the years with many wonderful clients and their families. I have been honored to be a part of so many lives as they struggled to find their way as strangers in the paradise they inhabit. I have learned as much from them as whatever they learned from me. I also have been blessed to work with some of the kindest, most caring advisors in the financial services industry, including Abacus Planning Group, Ballentine Partners, Signature, and Tolleson Wealth Management, among others. I hope *Strangers in Paradise* reflects back to them the patterns that emerged in working with them and their clients. Each provided a piece of the puzzle.

I also want to acknowledge the very kind and thoughtful Malcolm Gladwell. Our serendipitous encounter in 2011, and our contacts since then for his book *David and Goliath: Underdogs, Misfits, and the Art of Battling Giants* (2013, Little, Brown and Company), encouraged me to realize these ideas could be truly eye-opening for the general public.

I want to thank the many members of my publishing team who transformed all the bits and pieces into the book you hold in your hands. My editor, Susan Reynolds, provided invaluable structure, encouragement, and guidance as I made every mistake a rookie writer can make. The book design by Michael Gibbs and Valerie Brewster brought the content alive in a beautiful, elegant presentation. Behind it all has been my hardworking, intelligent, humorous office manager, Susan Eckstrom. She helped manage the project, encouraged me when I faltered, and told me when I needed to rest.

My deepest appreciation is reserved for my family, my own little group of Immigrants and Natives. I want to thank my parents, Simon and Sally, survivors of the Holocaust, whose resilience in creating a life in America formed my personal understanding of immigration, acculturation, and adaptation. My children—Joshua, Jeremy, and Joanna— are the renewal of a family that was nearly extinguished. I am so proud of each of my children for who they are as people. They, their loving relationships, and now the third generation just coming forth are the fulfillment of so many dreams.

Finally, behind everything stands Jeanne, my beautiful wife and devoted companion for nearly forty years. Without her love and support, nothing would be possible.

I

Immigration

CHAPTER 1

Immigrants to Wealth

Imagine for a moment that you have had the good fortune to immigrate to *paradise*, a land you'd heard about, read about, dreamed about, and longed to reach. This paradise is a land where an abundance of money creates opportunities to live much more comfortably, with more choices, than you ever experienced, including opportunities to be charitable to others and generous to your children.

Now imagine that this paradise came with a few special conditions:

- 80 percent of its citizens will have been born and raised elsewhere, like you.

- Immigrants will have to learn new rules, new responsibilities, and even some new language, all of which require special knowledge. Although there will be many guides around who say they can help, truly experienced guides will be difficult to find.

- Some newcomers will barely be welcomed and will soon feel isolated.

- Family and friends back home will not know how to handle the change in relationships with the few who made it to paradise.

- Due to common mistakes immigrants make in raising families, most of their native-born children or grandchildren will end up deported back to harsher lands.

- Convinced that such abundance is corrupting, some immigrant parents will *intentionally* send their children back to a life of hardship.

- Of the natives who do remain, life may be an emotional struggle.

- A fortunate few will learn what it takes to prosper, but their ways will be a mystery to most incoming immigrants and their families.

This land may now sound less inviting than you thought. Oddly enough, this paradise does exist. It's populated by those who achieve substantial wealth in America.

For the purposes of this discussion, we'll call this *paradise* the "Land of Wealth." From the perspective of working- and middle-class society, the Land of Wealth looks idyllic. But for those who migrate there, the list of caveats becomes very real and very challenging. They soon find themselves engaged in a battle to beat the odds of encountering the likeliest outcomes: getting deported back to economic hardship, or of staying in a fortunate yet potentially debilitating place. And since they arrive without a clear idea of the complexity that lies ahead and no roadmap to guide their way, many immigrants to wealth end up feeling imperiled. They very much feel like they are *strangers in paradise*.

Consider, if you will, the fates of three such immigrants, whose journeys we will follow throughout this book:

———

Phil Spinelli[1] felt his attention drift as his flight from Chicago began its long descent toward the Cleveland airport. Still half in shock from the signing the previous morning, he felt he'd left part of his life behind at the law firm's conference table. He quietly wondered: What have I done?

When Phil glanced to his left at Max Morgan, chief executive officer of their company SteriMetrix, Max's face possessed the same grin that had appeared when they signed the buyout papers. Max had come a long way from that small, depressed town he grew up in, thought Phil. But then again, Max had always made the effort to dress like a CEO, even in the company's early days. Well, Max could afford whatever he wanted now.

I guess I can, too, Phil realized, as if from a distance.

Phil leaned forward slightly to check on Joan Lloyd, their chief financial officer, who sat in the aisle seat. She was still wearing the same pale gray suit she'd worn to most business meetings for the past two years. Even though she gave Phil a half-smile back, her hands were gripping the arms of her seat. He'd noticed her frown of worry three months earlier, when they first received the initial call proposing the sale of SteriMetrix to a Midwestern *Fortune 100* conglomerate. Phil knew it wasn't just the complexity of all the financials that weighed on Joan. He knew she would also have to navigate how she and her husband Ted would cope with becoming multimillionaires. They had always been "proud to live very prudently." Phil thought "penny-pinching" was more accurate. He gave Joan a thumbs-up, hoping to bolster her courage for what was to come.

At fifty-two, Phil was the youngest of the three business partners. He had been hired as chief operating officer (COO) of SteriMetrix seven years prior, to help manage their surgical-instrument manufacturing facilities and oversee their valuable list of patents. This combination of high-margin specialty products and unique intellectual property eventually drew the big fish they had hoped to attract someday.

And now, within ninety days, the three partners would split the proceeds of the sale. As primary shareholder, Max would be netting $47 million in cash and stock in the parent company. Phil would net roughly $37 million in similar form, and Joan $20 million. After a one-year transition in consultant roles, they could begin diversifying out of the stock into whatever investments they chose, and they would be free to move on. If Phil wished, he could be more than comfortably retired at age fifty-three.

Phil and his wife Barb had whispered to each other many times over the past month, "That's a huge amount of money, $37 million." They had started to worry about how it would affect their children, twenty-three-year-old Gina and little ten-year-old Stephanie. That kind of money could change people, ruin children. Phil and Barb had known a few people who had become wealthy over the years through business or investments, but not anybody they could talk to about the personal side. The wealth felt overwhelming.

The commercial jet lurched slightly as the rear wheels hit the runway, then gently settled to the ground. Phil's sense of unreality, of still being in transit, seemed stronger, as if he had landed in a foreign country after departing from home only three days ago. He felt somehow like he should be going through Customs.

———

The Real Nature of Wealth

I am a psychologist working in the specialty field of wealth counseling and consulting. I have been helping individuals, couples, and families of wealth for nearly twenty years. A kindred spirit has been my wonderful colleague and collaborator, Dr. Dennis Jaffe, who has been providing consulting services to family businesses and families of wealth for over thirty years. We each have worked with hundreds of clients facing the many stresses that occur when families achieve great fortunes or work side-by-side in highly successful family-owned businesses. We have seen families—who *seem* to have it all—genuinely struggle with the fact that having wealth necessitates greater harmony and growth. In each of our consulting practices, Dennis and I often pondered why adjusting to wealth proves so difficult, and why so many who fail to adapt to the new reality of their lives lose the wealth, if not for themselves, then for their families.

One of the most compelling facts Dennis and I encountered years ago is that approximately 80 percent of the wealthy are not raised with wealth. Born within the world of working-, middle-, or even upper-middle-class life, 80 percent of those who acquire significant wealth formed their core identity in the economic culture of their upbringing, not within the culture of wealth. This reality exerts a profound effect on their ability to adapt to becoming wealthy. Their family life, their history, their self-image, even their understanding of wealth itself originated in economic conditions that didn't prepare them for the very real challenges and responsibilities that come with wealth.

In thinking through this pattern, Dennis and I arrived at a remarkable realization: Those who achieve wealth over the course of their lifetime make a journey to wealth, one that very much resembles that of ethnic or geographic immigrants disembarking on the shores of a new land.

Whether through business success over the course of decades or seemingly overnight through marriage or a financial windfall, newly wealthy individuals, couples, and families make a life-altering transition. Their journey is as real and as challenging to navigate as any migration from one country to another.

But, there is a fundamental problem. Because they arrived unprepared, and because the Land of Wealth is far more complicated than most people envision, these immigrants to wealth become, at heart, strangers in paradise.

The 80/20 Pattern

To fully understand the metaphor of "immigration to wealth," let's discuss one of the most curious aspects of wealth, namely, *the 80/20 Pattern*. Over the past thirty years, various surveys have been published analyzing who is wealthy in America. These surveys generally set out to determine some set of characteristics, ranging from what the wealthy worry about to which investments are of greatest interest. Most of these surveys begin by asking a fundamental question of the respondents: What is the source of your wealth: Self-made? Windfall? Inheritance? Some combination of inheritance and personal success? The survey results are then analyzed in light of the various demographic groups, noting findings such as, "48 percent of those with self-made wealth feel their kids are already spoiled" or some equally dramatic but not-so-meaningful statistic.

For decades, these studies have identified the same three groups:

- The largest group by far, *around 75 percent to 85 percent,* reports having acquired wealth as a result of investment success, business development, marriage, or perhaps a financial windfall. They achieved wealth after having grown up in lesser economic circumstances, such as working- or middle-class life.

- A small group, perhaps 5 percent to 10 percent, reports the main source of their wealth as inheritance or from growing up in a wealthy family.

- The remaining group of 10 percent to 15 percent is a mixed group. Their wealth is derived partly from inheritance and partly from self-made success or significant growth of the money they received.

These basic proportions surface again and again, in study after study, at any level of wealth you may imagine.

This means that approximately 80 percent of the wealthy have come to their wealth in their lifetime. They are newcomers, what's known in the vernacular as New Money. Very few of the wealthy are Old Money, far fewer than most tend to think.

Wealth in America

- A survey by US Trust in 2006 of those with $5 million or more in investable wealth found that 84 percent of respondents: "Had to start from scratch, or became wealthy later in life"[2]

- A 2008 PNC Wealth Management survey of those with $500,000 to over $1 million in investable wealth reported that 89 percent earned their wealth. Only 8 percent owed their wealth to inheritance alone.[3] In 2012, a similar PNC survey of millionaires found 75 percent had come from a middle-class background while 12 percent "grew up well off or wealthy." In a rarely reported statistic, 12 percent had come from poverty or a working-class environment.[4]

- In a recent study of upper-income professionals, approximately 74 percent came from lower- or middle-class socioeconomic backgrounds.[5] Of the remaining 26 percent citing some degree of upper-middle-class heritage, a mere 4 percent came from a truly wealthy upbringing.

- Most people assume that *Forbes Magazine's* list of the 400 richest Americans, first published in 1982, is populated largely by members who inherited wealth as opposed to earning their wealth. As recently as the mid-1990s, this was fairly accurate, with 48 percent of the 1997 *Forbes 400* achieving their position largely due to inheritance.[6] But the proportion possessing solely inherited wealth has shrunk to only about a quarter of the list,[7] a level closer to the general pattern of wealth in the US population.[8] Approximately 75 percent are now predominantly self-made billionaires or entrepreneurs who grew their inheritance to a much larger fortune.

The Ticking Clock

Dennis Jaffe and I knew another key fact from our experience in wealth counseling: From the moment an individual or family is able to enter the Land of Wealth, the clock starts ticking on their eventual departure. While immigration to economic paradise is very hard, eventual deportation is virtually guaranteed for all but a few who successfully adapt.

Consider for a moment the 80/20 pattern noted above. More than a pattern, it is a paradox. Given that a constant stream of economic immigrants is pouring into the Land of Wealth, mostly from middle-class life, the population statistics should gradually show a change over time. The land should swell with immigrants putting down roots, raising families, and growing communities of native-born citizens, much like what occurs in America herself. The ranks of those with inherited wealth should rise proportionally, as established residents. More and more inhabitants should be native-born citizens, many generations removed from their immigrant forebears.

Yet, the ranks of the wealthy in America generally grow at a modest pace—about 6–8 percent per year on average over the past several decades.[9] This growth depends more on economic conditions and the rise of the value of investments and business than on any major influx of newcomers. If anything, the growing income-inequality gap of the past decade has made it harder than ever to migrate to wealth from middle-class life.

The implication is ominous: People are streaming out of the metaphorical Land of Wealth at a much faster pace than they are pouring in. Only by this massive exodus could the 80/20 proportion of acquirers outnumbering inheritors remain in place, by so wide a margin, so consistently, over so long a period of time.

The reasons for this pattern are partially associated with economic factors. These include the rate of business creation and destruction, the fragile nature of investment success, and the calculus of supporting a rapidly proliferating family tree from a slowly growing financial fortune. The effects of taxes, advisory fees, and potentially subpar performance of investments, wracked by the occasional economic downturn, also play a role.

The most powerful factor, however, is not economic. It has to do with the family dynamics associated with wealth.

Why Wealth Disappears

Society has generally known that wealth is tenuous. This knowledge is deeply encoded in proverbs about wealth around the globe, captured by the saying in Western culture as "shirtsleeves to shirtsleeves in three generations."[10] Each culture has its version of the proverb that wealth is built by the first generation, enjoyed by the second generation, and squandered by the third generation: "From the stalls to the stars to the stalls" in Italy; "rice paddy to rice paddy in three generations" in Asia; "merchant grandfather, noble father, beggar son" in Spain; and "there's nothing but three generations between clogs and clogs" in Ireland.

The nature of wealth itself is usually blamed. We are sure that money corrupts, or that the power money has will corrupt those who own it. We are positive that having riches brings out the greed in people in an ever-increasing cycle of destruction. We are sure it is about the money.

It is not. The reality is this: Immigrants to wealth arrive unprepared for the world they encounter. Without guidelines to help adapt to their new economic culture, the majority of these immigrants struggle, stumble, and ultimately fail to adapt, effectively deporting themselves and their heirs from paradise.

———

On Max's way home from the airport he stopped at his wife's favorite jeweler and bought her a very expensive pair of diamond earrings. He knew Adrienne would love them. He also knew that a part of her expected it. Coming in the door, Adrienne threw her arms around him and shouted, "We're rich! We're rich!" Max grinned widely and then kissed her. He was so happy for himself and for her. They had finally arrived. What they did not consider was whether, after living just beyond their income for much of their life together, they had the financial and emotional skills to handle what was about to happen.

———

Expanding the Metaphor

The immigration-to-wealth metaphor opened the door to several groundbreaking ideas about why families of wealth so rarely succeed. Each of these insights were so powerful in their own right that, together, they helped explain why maintaining wealth across even one generation is very hard, let alone sustaining wealth across multiple generations.

WEALTH'S IMMIGRANTS FACE A COMPLEX ADJUSTMENT

Dennis and I realized that when people become wealthy, they must learn, as individuals, to adjust to the *unique culture* of wealth, with its new customs and new responsibilities. Ethnic immigrants must naturally find ways to adjust to the unfamiliar culture to which they migrate. So too must wealth's newcomers negotiate a complex interplay between their old habits, attitudes, beliefs, and behaviors and their new experiences, behaviors, customs, and language.

Like many ethnic immigrants, the newly wealthy attempt to adapt largely by making guesses, extrapolating from what they believe, what they've been told, and what they have experienced. The problem is that what most people think they know about wealth typically comes from friends or family, movies, books, magazines, TV shows, and the Internet. Most of that information does not come from those who actually live in the Land of Wealth.

If the newly wealthy are lucky, they learn quickly by trial and error or by listening to whatever guidance they may receive from fellow travelers. Unfortunately, even these solutions rely on guesses, many of which are off the mark and ultimately damaging, particularly to the way the family learns to function in their new circumstances. Some cling to outmoded beliefs too long while others abandon cherished values too quickly. And all too many keep silent when they should be asking for directions and talking to each other about the journey.

———

When Joan arrived home from the Chicago meeting, she found Ted in the garage changing the oil in their old sedan. His father had drummed into him that it was better to take care of what you have than to buy into "the throwaway culture of American life." Ted also liked keeping his hands busy when he was working out stress in his head.

After Joan described the signing ceremony, Ted congratulated her by offering a sour smile as he wiped his hands on a greasy rag. They looked at each other for a moment, then Joan asked in a quiet voice, "What are we going do about the money?" Ted shook his head once and replied, "We're not going to touch it. No need to."

They spent the next ten minutes talking about the situation. Both felt that leading a simple, frugal life fit their values and their habits. Despite the dramatic alteration in the family's finances, they didn't want to change much. They both felt that nothing good came of being rich.

———

THE GREATEST MISTAKE MANY NEWCOMERS MAKE IS THAT THEY believe they already know the roadmap for adapting to wealth—but they would be wrong. Their economic background has simply not prepared them for the complexity of what they will face. No matter how smart they are, living intelligently with wealth is not easily deduced. Living within the Land of Wealth must be understood through eyes attuned to a culture very different than middle-class life. It takes time, thoughtfulness, and openness to learning new strategies for navigating this new environment successfully.

PREPARING THE CHILDREN IS PARAMOUNT

The second implication of the immigration-to-wealth metaphor is even more powerful. Even if the wealth-acquirer makes a suitable adaptation to the Land of Wealth, he or she is still faced with one of the most daunting tasks of immigrant life: *How do I raise children successfully in a culture in which I myself was not raised?*

Because 80 percent of the wealthy arise from lesser economic circumstances, they have no history of handling wealth in families. They have no mental template, no map for how to parent children in the context of wealth. Parenting is difficult enough under normal circumstances. Parenting in a foreign land adds levels of stress and risk that can derail a family.

Wealth's immigrants must somehow accomplish the impossible: They must navigate the tricky path of their own adjustment to a new culture, while simultaneously shepherding those children and grand-children under their care to be healthy native-born citizens of that culture. If not well-prepared for managing wealth in all its complexity, those generations will become their own version of strangers in para-dise, even though it is their homeland.

The stakes for raising families in a culture of wealth are therefore very high, higher than in situations of ethnic immigration from one country to another. With wealth, each generation must renew its cit-izenship—they must remain wealthy. Each generation must have the wherewithal for managing and living with wealth successfully, not just by holding onto or growing their financial fortune, but by being psy-chologically prepared for the culture they inhabit. Without that prep-aration, the family will begin the all-too-inevitable journey back to middle-class life.

Roadmap for a New Territory

The metaphor of "Immigrants and Natives to wealth"* was only the beginning of understanding wealth in families from a new perspec-tive. Pursuing the idea led me to examine more deeply the field of cross-cultural psychology, a field that has been examining the genera-tional strengths and stresses of ethnic and geographic immigrants for decades. I soon realized how many of the field's longstanding concepts, research, and predictions are highly applicable to wealth in families. I also saw how these could provide a new roadmap for successful accul-turation to the Land of Wealth.

Oddly enough, cross-cultural psychology has never turned its own spotlight on the cultural aspects of wealth in families. It has tradi-tionally seen economic class as just one variable among many used to

---

* From this point forward, capitalized references to Immigrants or Natives will refer to economic acquirers or inheritors in the Land of Wealth using the metaphor of the book. Lower-case spelling of immigrants or natives will refer to ethnic groups or general cross-cultural psychology terms.

describe the lives of individuals and families. For the first time, in this book, the metaphor Dennis Jaffe and I originally formulated is being applied to wealth as a culture in and of itself. This model is truly a unique approach that shifts the light just so, suddenly illuminating a striking new perspective.

In this book, you and I will examine together the formidable journey of adaptation for wealth's Immigrants and Natives, guided by the amazing parallels to families who make an ethnic migration. Time and again, we shall discover how so much of what we have long believed about the wealthy is not about the money—it is about the cultural challenges facing those who come to wealth and those who are born to it.

A Guide for Everyone in the Land of Wealth

The more I have come to view my clients' lives through the lens of culture, rather than their economics or even social class,[11] the more I have come to understand and address what goes wrong in the process of "economic immigration." The concepts have resonated strongly with families struggling with the challenges of wealth, and the results have been transformative. My hope is that, through the knowledge conveyed in this book, many more families will learn how to adapt successfully to the paradise they worked so hard to reach.

Beyond the value for families, however, there are added benefits to understanding wealth through a cultural lens. This perspective offers professionals who work with the wealthy new strategies for helping their clients. For many families, trusted advisors serve as guides to the Land of Wealth. Yet most advisors to the wealthy are overwhelmingly either still middle class or newly arrived Immigrants to wealth themselves. This means they are making many of the same guesses, viewed through the same cultural attitudes, as the Immigrants they are charged with guiding. Put simply, economic paradise is a land in which predominantly middle-class people advise other predominantly middle-class people who just happen to have a lot of money.

By understanding the territory better, including the turning points where families stumble and fall along their journey, advisors to the wealthy will be able to approach their task with new, more nuanced skills for helping guide the way.

This perspective on wealth also comes at a time when the wealth culture itself is undergoing major transitions. Formerly a predominantly white male enclave, wealth is gradually incorporating more diverse populations in larger numbers than ever before. Particularly for the growing number of female executives, women-owned businesses, and next-generation daughters succeeding their wealth-creating fathers, the Land of Wealth is changing. In emerging economies and developed nations around the world, new members of the middle class are making their own migration upwards to become part of global wealth. These transformations are significantly impacting the cultural norms defining wealth in the US and around the world. A cultural perspective about the lives of wealthy families is especially timely.

In the following chapters, we shall examine together the following landmarks and pathways related to wealth:

- What constitutes the Land of Wealth and the nature of its inhabitants;

- Acculturation: how newcomers personally adjust to becoming wealthy, including the crucial choices that set the direction for the family, for better or worse; and, finally,

- Adaptation: how families must make their own choices across generations to build the competencies required with wealth.

For families and advisors alike, the hope is simple yet profound: to transform the many Immigrants and Natives in the Land of Wealth into resilient, productive citizens who no longer have to feel like *Strangers in Paradise*.

CHAPTER 2

The Land of Wealth

To understand wealth's citizenry, we must first know some basics about the territory they inhabit.

———

Max Morgan and his wife Adrienne liked to live well on his salary as Steri-Metrix's CEO. He had worked hard to get where he was, first as the young owner of a small machine shop and then as founding partner of what would become a successful precision manufacturing company.

Max had grown up in a poor section of Cleveland. His parents and four brothers and sisters shared a small apartment over the neighborhood convenience store his father struggled to keep afloat. His father would rail bitterly against the landlord who was quick to collect rent payments but slow to maintain the rundown block of storefronts. His mother always looked depleted. They ate when the store did well; they went hungry when money dried up. After years of overhearing his parents argue about money, Max decided that good times and lean times came unpredictably, so you'd better enjoy life while things were good.

With a head for numbers and intuitive mechanical ability, Max snagged a full-time scholarship to Ohio State. He left for college committed to becoming a success in the world. But despite Max's knack for business finance, in his personal life he could never discipline himself to build up much of a nest egg. When his bank balance would reach a certain point, he'd treat himself to sharp clothes and whatever American muscle car the salesman could talk him into buying. He understood salary, not savings, and he trusted his abilities. He already was living better than his parents had ever experienced. He figured there'd be plenty of time to save once he was rich.

———

What Is Wealth?

For most people struggling within the limitations of working- or middle-class wages, fine distinctions about how much money it takes to be truly wealthy seem like absurd hair-splitting. Objective measures of wealth, such as "investable net worth," can be quite literally foreign concepts to middle-class society, who sees them as part of the language and culture of a distant land.

When asked what it takes to "be rich," most non-wealthy people give one of the following subjective responses that relate either to being freed from money problems or able to focus on their values:[12]

- Getting paid one year's income all at once.
- Being able to pay off all my debt.
- Having more money than everyone around me.
- Not having to worry about whether I can afford something.
- Being able to buy whatever I want without thinking about it first.
- Being able to give as much as I want to charity.
- Being able to help my family and friends as much as I want.
- Being able to retire comfortably.

Although mainly subjective, these measures are entirely valid as thresholds to a financially relaxed life. What's important to note is that, with the possible exception of "having more money than everyone around you" (a measure many of the wealthy also cite), these benchmarks are grounded in the scarcity, anxiety, and insecurity shared by people raised in the lower or middle class. A life of abundance exists *out there*, beyond the border of middle-class life—in what they view as financial paradise. Just as citizens of a war-torn country, who live with constant danger, scarce food, and a dictatorial government, long for a place of peace, prosperity, and plenty, most of society longs for the safe haven of wealth.

Once on the inside, however, the Land of Wealth does have objective, definable borders. Knowing these is important for understanding the cultural perspectives that are initially foreign to its Immigrants and natural to its Natives.

Measuring Wealth

Like any country or culture, the Land of Wealth consists of different regions. Some are just over the border from middle-class territory, where the landscape opens up to a glimpse of paradise, the air is fresher, life is easier, and the financial insecurities of middle-class life diminish. This is the land of the top 10 percent of economic households, which, in the United States, includes the fortunate souls with ownership (net worth) of nearly $1 million or more.[13] A bit deeper into the territory of wealth reside those households whose net worth approaches $7–$8 million, placing them at the top 1 percent in the US. From there, the land rises sharply to much greener hills, encompassing the top one-half of one percent, the top one-tenth of one percent, and the very rarefied air of the billionaire *Forbes 400* list, where the average net worth in 2012 was $4.2 billion.

Measures of wealth vary more than most people realize, so understanding who is wealthy is not as simple as it might appear. Within the culture of wealth, particularly among advisors to wealth, the three main ways to define wealth are:

- Annual income: the flow of money coming in on a regular basis from any source for spending and other purposes, such as saving, investing, and charity.
- Total net worth: the sum of an individual's assets minus his or her debts and liabilities, what someone owns minus what they owe.
- Investable net worth, not including the value of one's primary home: the pool of financial assets available to manage as investments, not counting the value of one's primary residence.

ANNUAL INCOME

Yearly income is the money measure most people from a working-class or middle-class background know. Whatever is coming into the household is all that is available to spend, save, or donate. Yet annual income is actually the least reliable—or important—measure when it comes to thinking about real wealth.

A simple analogy may help. If we compare money to water, *income* would be what comes out of the faucets in our homes, available for everyday use. If what is coming in exceeds what we use, we might divert the overflow to a water tank or reservoir on our property for storage. That would constitute an *asset,* a reserve akin to a savings account, perhaps. Both income flow and asset reserves face risks to their stability. But proper management of a good reservoir of assets protects us from the vagaries that can slow or shut off precious cash flow.

Median household income in the US hovers around the $50,000 level.[14] For many people, expenses deplete most of that, leaving little left over. There is very little stored away, often because there is insufficient income to allow for savings.[15] Income is all that many households have. More importantly, managing income is all that the majority of American households know about money.

Because of the middle class's strong orientation to income, the government mostly focuses on annual income when conducting surveys. Thus, many economic studies report wealth in terms of annual income. As of 2012, a household annual income of around $150,000 qualified as the gateway to the top 10 percent of earners. A bit farther into the Land of Wealth marked the top 1 percent of annual income, where those with an annual income of $521,000 or more live.[16] For someone struggling to make ends meet at or below the $50,000 annual income mark, a half-million dollars per year in income certainly would feel like paradise.

THE NEED TO FOCUS ON ASSETS, NOT INCOME

What divides many working- and middle-class earners from wealth holders is the recognition that income is not typically the best means for creating or preserving real wealth. Water gushing out of the faucet may be wonderful. But, the city could experience a drought, a water main could break, or the well could run dry. From a financial perspective, income is vulnerable to job stability, investment results, one-time sales of businesses or real estate, and tax laws.

Building up a reservoir of assets provides the safety, security, and opportunity that form a sense of abundance. Assets are what determine the family's ability to migrate to the Land of Wealth.

Money is so limited in many middle-class families that, even if the family does experience an increase in income, they may use it rather than store it. They may choose to pay down debt, for example, or make long-overdue repairs to their car or their house. Most families raised in middle-class life are essentially unfamiliar with handling large stores of wealth. Being unfamiliar with asset management, they are unprepared for it, until and unless they seek training.

Most Americans have no more than two major assets: the value of their home and the level of their retirement account. The size of these assets is typically quite modest and not easily converted to cash (they are *illiquid*). In 2010, the median home value was $170,000 but, subtracting for mortgage debt, provided only around $55,000 in home equity.[17] The median retirement account, for people over the age of forty-five, holds between $60,000 to $100,000.[18] So compared to even modest levels of wealth, those arising from middle-class culture are used to handling money in the tens- or hundreds-of-thousands of dollars range, a very different level of money management than having millions of dollars. As such, middle-class Immigrants' prior financial experience may provide few of the money management skills they will need as they migrate to wealth.

Strangers new to owning wealth have to learn, possibly for the first time in their lives, that they must pay attention less to what's coming out of the faucet and more to the gleaming new reservoir that must sustain the family. They must learn the complex interplay among asset management, income from multiple sources, cash flow, and management of some type of capital reserve for unexpected or unusual expenditures (what most people know as an emergency fund or savings account). They must also avoid the temptation to ramp up their spending to match the income pouring in. Otherwise, their newfound wealth will just go down a bigger drain, leaving little left over to replenish their reserves.

To remain successfully in the Land of Wealth, Immigrants must learn these skills or address them indirectly through wise selection of advisors. Eventually, they must also teach these skills to their children and grandchildren. Failure to do any of these steps risks depleting the reservoir, sending the family back to relying upon whatever income comes out of the tap.

———

For weeks after the signing, Max and Adrienne felt like they were walking on air, a strange but very pleasant kind of shock. As she pushed her

shopping cart around in her local Target, Adrienne kept thinking to herself, we are going to be really rich. Here I am, and no one knows I'm
going to have millions and millions. She wondered if she somehow
looked or acted differently, given how differently she felt.

Max felt the same way at work. As the logistics of the sale moved
forward, people in the office asked him what he was going to do once
the post-sale requirements had been met. He said, "Retirement, here I
come!" He and Adrienne started talking to builders and architects about
designing their dream home. One morning, before coming into the company, he went down to talk to his favorite car salesman about picking
colors for his new Corvette.

TOTAL NET WORTH VERSUS INVESTABLE NET WORTH

As recently as the year 2000, an individual needed to have only $1 mil-
lion in total net worth (assets minus liabilities) to reach the top 1 percent or 2 percent of wealth holders in the US population. Just twelve
years later, with inflation and the growth of wealth in America, that
same $1 million barely qualified for entrance to the top eight percent
of wealth-holders in the country.

For society at large, this transformation has gone largely unnoticed. TV shows like "Who Wants to Be a Millionaire?" and stories in
mass-market publications, such as USA Today,[19] reveal that most people still consider anyone worth $1 million to "have arrived." Indeed, to
the average American, $1 million in net worth constitutes a huge step
up the economic ladder. Those worth $1 million may also feel they may
have crossed the border into the Land of Wealth, but they will soon be
acutely aware that other residents possess much greater claim to the territory. One recent study surveyed millionaires on how much money it
would take to "feel rich."[20] Over half of the respondents identified the
$7 million to $8 million range as the start of "real wealth." They were not
that wrong; this is currently the entry point to the top 1 percent of net
worth. Within only a few years, that threshold will require $10 million.

So what is the best measure of wealth? Net worth is the basic accounting measure of all our assets minus all our debts and other liabilities.
However, this broad measure includes one major flaw: the value of

the home we live in, our *primary residence*. This is problematic in several ways. While once considered fairly stable and likely to rise annually, home values are subject to significant variations, as the events of the past decade have so painfully demonstrated. Home values are also notoriously affected by local or regional norms; compare the cost of a two-bedroom house in Mobile, Alabama, with a similar home in Silicon Valley, California. Plus, most American homeowners have a significant degree of mortgage debt offsetting the value of the house. Other than taking out a home equity loan to raise cash, a home is not a liquid asset available for paying expenses or making purchases.

Investable net worth not including primary residence is therefore the best measure of economic level, even though this measure is the least well known outside the Land of Wealth. Investable net worth represents the amount of money an individual or household has to invest, grow, use for charity or special expenditures, and pass on as inheritance. It doesn't include the value of one's home and is independent of income.

Using this measure, nearly 3.5 million households in the US now have $1 million dollars or more in investable net worth.[21] This is a larger number than most people realize. If all those with at least $1 million in investable assets were gathered in one place, it would create the third largest city in the United States, behind New York City and Los Angeles, but ahead of Chicago.[22]

Regions in the Land of Wealth

———

Joan's financial expertise at work carried over only moderately to their personal financial management. At home, because she and Ted didn't plan on doing anything with their windfall, they saw little need to do any intricate investing for their wealth.

In the years before SteriMetrix was sold, Joan had been earning a six-figure annual income with big annual bonuses. To avoid Ted's reactions to her earning so much more than he did as an appliance store manager, Joan told him she earned a good salary but not that she received such big bonuses. She would have the checks direct-deposited alongside the rest of their money without mentioning them to Ted.

The Lloyds owned a modest house for which they no longer had any mortgage. As a result of high income, low spending, and conservative investments within local bank and brokerage accounts, they had amassed $2.7 million before the $20 million from the SteriMetrix sale. Anyone visiting the Lloyds's home or observing their lifestyle would have assumed they were a typical middle-class household having to be careful about paying the bills.

—

ONCE AN INDIVIDUAL CROSSES THE THRESHOLD OF HAVING $1 MIL-lion in investable assets, they encounter a very large territory with different regions of wealth. These have significant implications for the lives of families who migrate to paradise. The Capgemini/RBC World Wealth Report has traditionally separated the wealthy into three levels:

- Millionaire High-Net-Worth (HNW) Individuals: Individuals with investable wealth between $1 million and $5 million.
- Mid-Tier Millionaires: Individuals with investable wealth between $5 million and $30 million.
- Ultra-High-Net-Worth (UHNW) Individuals: Individuals with investable net worth over $30 million.

If the Land of Wealth literally encompassed geographic regions with resident populations, it would hold sizable cities. That Mid-Tier level between $5 million and $30 million comprises about 400,000 individuals, equivalent to the population of Miami, Florida. This tier stretches across a very wide span of wealth. As a result, wealth-holders in that Mid-Tier range are often divvied up by various surveys, financial publications, wealth management firms, and luxury-goods providers into either the high-net-worth (HNW) or ultra-high-net worth (UHNW) range. Some would consider a person with $15 million to be UHNW, while many others would see them as being "only" HNW.

More than 55,000 people—half the capacity of the University of Michigan football stadium—have greater than $30 million in investable net worth in America, including the *Forbes 400* members who possess between $2.5 billion and $60 billion as of the 2012 version of the list.[23]

Differing Perspectives on the Land of Wealth

Those who live, work, and provide services within the culture of wealth have a distinct perspective on the numbers that denote wealth, compared to people from other economic cultures. This is no different than perspectives about one country or culture when seen from the outside versus the inside. If you come from Greece, or China, or Paraguay, you may be more likely to hold views about Americans *in general*, rather than understanding important regional or ethnic differences between the people in New Hampshire, New Mexico, and New York. Living within the middle class—or, more importantly, migrating from the middle class—carries a set of views about the wealthy based on what's believed *outside* the Land of Wealth. Upon arrival and settlement into economic paradise, those views may be severely challenged.

Several things to keep in mind are:

1. For wealth's many Immigrants, your view of where you are in the Land of Wealth depends greatly on where you are from, where you now stand, and how far and fast you have traveled to get there. You also may be acutely aware of how you arrived.

2. For those Natives born and raised within the Land of Wealth, you may or may not know where you are, depending on what you've been told and what you discover. More importantly, your future depends on how prepared you are to live in your homeland.

Next, we'll discuss the inhabitants of the Land of Wealth.

CHAPTER 3

Immigrants and Natives

Those looking in from outside typically identify the inhabitants of the Land of Wealth with one common label: "The Rich." This is no different than the way residents of the United States may be lumped together as "those Americans" by other countries. Stamping the label "The Rich" on the wealthy removes their identities and individual differences. It also creates a false impression of homogeneity, that they are all the same. This is far from the truth.

People become citizens of the Land of Wealth the same as in any country: They travel there as Immigrants, or are born there as Natives. Immigrants may make the journey slowly, developing wealth over a period of five, ten, twenty years, or more. Or, they may arrive with stunning rapidity, as when they marry a multi-millionaire, inherit the fortune of a long-lost uncle, or win the lottery. Native-born citizens, on the other hand, are raised within the culture of affluence and understand its language, customs, and attitudes.[24]

More often than most people realize, both Immigrants and Natives to wealth still feel like strangers in paradise long after they've established a home base. A first step toward understanding their situations is to understand the key differences in how they are identified within the Land of Wealth.

Immigrants to Wealth

Most denizens of the Land of Wealth are, as they say in Maine, "from Away." They arise from working-, middle-, or even upper-middle-class culture.[25] In the vocabulary of cross-cultural psychology, where they came from is their *home or heritage* economic culture, within which the foundation of their identity and personality was forged. The Land of

Wealth is their *receiving, adoptive,* or *host* culture, the one to which they must successfully adapt if they want their families to prosper emotionally and financially.[26] The complex process of making this adjustment on a personal level is termed *acculturation.*[27]

Cross-cultural psychology recognizes a multitude of immigrant subtypes: voluntary and involuntary migrants, short-term sojourners, asylum seekers, refugees, international students, and expatriates, to name the most common. Similar subtypes exist for economic immigrants.

PIONEERS: CREATORS OF FORTUNES

Immigrants who make the long journey to wealth through hard work and perseverance are very much the Pioneers in paradise. They create businesses, alone or with family members, invest successfully in real estate or financial markets, or earn high salaries which they save and invest instead of spend. Pioneers' economic success may grow gradually over many years, or it may blossom suddenly after a period of nurturing. The business owner who sells his or her company for a large profit (as our examples Phil, Max, and Joan did) or who gets a massive infusion of cash by taking a company public experiences what is termed a *liquidity event.* The heretofore locked-up value of the business is transformed into investable wealth. Other examples include the many sports celebrities, actors, or artists who labor for years developing their craft, and then become "overnight successes" with high-dollar contracts or income. Pioneers are noted by their sense of having earned the wealth through their own effort, often after a long, arduous journey. Moreover, others tend to believe that Pioneers deserve their entrance to the Land of Wealth, due to their hard work and personal contribution to becoming successful.

TRANSPLANTS: RECIPIENTS OF GOOD FORTUNE

In contrast to the purposeful journeys of Pioneers, some Immigrants arrive nearly overnight. They may do so by means of a windfall, such as winning the lottery or getting a large financial settlement from litigation. Or, they are ushered in through relationship with a person of wealth, such as by marriage, kinship, or as a member of a stepfamily. Unlike Pioneers, Transplants' migration is more often viewed as luck, good fortune, God's will, or fortunate attachment to someone successful. Though Transplants may feel ecstatic about their entrance to economic paradise, they may also struggle because they (or others) believe they didn't really *earn* their visa. They also may be reeling from the suddenness of their uprooting and migration to wealth, as with lottery winners who catapult from working-class to millionaire status literally overnight.

Natives of Wealth

In contrast to the many Immigrants reaching the Land of Wealth, Natives are born there. These are the children, grandchildren, and great-grandchildren born into wealth-owning families, exposed to an affluent environment during their growth and development. They experience living, traveling, taking vacations, socializing, and being educated with at least some degree of wealth. Unlike Immigrants, Natives are likely to identify with the world of wealth. Equally important, people aware of their Native status definitely view them as part of the wealth culture.

Natives may work or spend much of their time in activities associated with other wealthy individuals and families as the normal course of their life. We hear of ultra-high-net-worth (UHNW) heirs who associate only with their own kind, doing activities only possible with extreme wealth, as documented in the video *Born Rich* by Johnson & Johnson heir Jamie Johnson.[28]

In reality, most Natives interface to a greater or lesser degree with the world of middle-class culture, despite the significant differences in their economic lives. Even though they or their parents are wealthy, many Natives live in an everyday world surrounded by middle-class people and activities. Living as a member of a demographically small minority group (the wealthy), embedded within a demographically more numerous majority culture (the middle class), is an important dynamic that Natives of wealth must be prepared to navigate. Their knowledge of different economic cultures doesn't draw from their own past, as it does for Immigrants. Their knowledge must draw from being exposed to how others live, in the present. They must learn, in this sense, to be bicultural, as we shall revisit in Chapter 8. Adapting to this difference is a challenge all its own.

Unlike Immigrants, Natives do not have a life experience of shifting from one cultural environment to another. Their heritage and adult citizenships are one and the same. They don't come "from Away," they are "from Here." Instead, people raised with wealth experience what they hope to be a stable and predictable life without any need for transition. Their biggest risk and deepest fear may be that there will be a transition *downward*, back into the middle-class world their parents or grandparents came from. They want to stay in the land of their birth, not get deported.

NATIVE, BUT NOT WEALTHY

The outside world assumes all next-generation members of wealthy families are wealthy themselves. Yet, despite what middle-class society may think, not all Natives of wealth are inheritors, and not all inheritors are Natives. Inheritance and Native status are not synonymous. Although most Natives someday do inherit family money and therefore can appropriately also be called inheritors, being a Native is a matter of cultural experience and identity, not a measure of personal financial worth.

Many Natives raised with wealth actually own or manage relatively little wealth themselves, either well until adulthood or throughout their entire lives. Because family money is tied up in trusts or other financial entities not under their control, many Natives *never* obtain full ownership of their money. This creates a state of limbo, akin to being a permanent resident of the Land of Wealth but without any naturalization papers. This feeling of suspension or disenfranchisement keeps many Natives' relationship with their family's money distant, passive, and perhaps resentful. Money arrives with little connection to its source. Ironically, it creates a situation analogous to that dependent mindset of thinking of money as income, rather than money as an asset to be carefully managed by one's own skills and decisions.

This experience of being a Native of wealth without actually controlling much wealth lessens the sense of ownership over one's money. It creates a little-recognized but genuine stress for many Natives. Imagine growing up in America and continuing to live and work in America, but never being a full citizen or having control over whether you could be deported at any time. You might be very appreciative of the privilege you've been granted. But you also may naturally develop other, more complex feelings of stress, resentment, passivity, and envy of those whose lives are fully their own.

Those individuals whose families once owned fortunes but no longer do so represent a more dramatic disconnection between Native status and wealth status. Their existence is familiar to society, even though it has never been framed so clearly in terms of culture. These are the stories of Old Money who, despite no longer being people *with* wealth, are still clearly seen as people *of* wealth. Novels and movies tell stories of multigenerational wealth-holders who lost their fortunes but retain the trappings of the culture of money: the language, the attitudes, the perspectives on other economic classes, the legacy of their ancestors, even the possessions and clothing of days gone by. These are the Natives of wealth who still clearly identify with wealth—and whom society identifies with wealth—but who now live a middle-class existence because the money is gone.

On a smaller level, this subset of Natives also represents the offspring of more modestly wealthy families who get returned to middle-class life when the math of inheritance divides the family's large reservoir into middle-class-sized tanks. Five grandchildren inheriting the remains of an $8 million estate, after taxes and fees, wind up back outside the border of the Land of Wealth, remembering what it was like but no longer citizens. As the 80/20 pattern about wealth tell us, these deportees from paradise are more plentiful than we think. They are the descendants of wealth's Immigrants who, due to a combination of economics and lack of preparation for remaining wealthy, wind up back in middle-class life and culture after the family's all-too-brief sojourn to wealth.

WEALTHY BUT NOT NATIVE

Similarly, not all inheritors are Natives of wealth. Many people who eventually inherit wealth were raised in middle-class homes, with no awareness or expectation of affluence and no experience with living affluently. They come to wealth at the grace of parents or other benefactors, at some point in adulthood, similar to that of a lottery windfall. With modern increases in longevity and the consequent delay in receiving inheritances until well into one's fifties or sixties, these middle-class inheritors are far more similar to Immigrant Transplants than Native inheritors. The moment of inheritance becomes an unexpected liquidity event for these individuals. This is particularly true for those in the second generation of families who shy away from using or showing whatever wealth they have accumulated (discussed in Chapter 5).

The lesson here is the opposite of the adage, "follow the money." It's not about how much money you have. It is about the way you grew up, in what culture. Culture determines where these inheritors feel they belong and the beliefs and attitudes that influence their life. Culture dictates whether they are prepared to handle wealth naturally or must adjust to a new world of having wealth. Being Native to wealth is about whether your heritage culture is one of affluence rather than middle-class. If it is, you are a Native. If it is not, you are an Immigrant.

Immigrant-Native Hybrids

There are two special groups who don't neatly fit into being clearly Immigrant or Native. Both are subsets of Natives, raised with some degree of affluence, who migrate during their lifetimes to higher levels of wealth. These Natives wind up having many Immigrant experiences and qualities.

NATIVES WHO EXPAND THE WEALTH

One subgroup consists of those Natives who either take charge of replenishing the family's depleted wealth or take their own inherited wealth and increase it significantly. Through entrepreneurship or skill in compounding the family's assets, these Natives essentially pick up and move the family farther into the Land of Wealth. This is that demographic subgroup in the studies of the wealthy whose source of wealth is labeled "partly inherited and partly self-made," constituting perhaps 10 percent of the wealth population.

To outsiders in middle-class society, this seems like a trivial difference: *The family was already rich, they are just richer now.* Yet for some families, the magnitude of this new change is as dramatic as the first migration from having a $45,000 annual income and $3,000 in the bank to a net worth of $5 million dollars. Growing up in an upper-middle-class home—as Bill Gates did—is still worlds apart from life as a multi-billionaire. The cultural adjustment is at least somewhat disorienting for the wealth-creator, and the lives of succeeding generations are transformed dramatically. Natives who enhance the family's fortune enjoy dual benefits. Like Pioneers, they rightfully possess a strong sense of accomplishment in earning greater wealth and in leading the family to a much better region in financial paradise. Yet they also began with a natural sense of the Land of Wealth. They do not start off feeling as strange in paradise. They already know the territory.

NATIVES WHO UNLOCK THE WEALTH

The other hybrid group consists of multigenerational families who have prospered for three, four, or five generations by operating very successful companies in their industries, but whose wealth is largely tied up in the business. For decades, some executives are paid well and enjoy access to significant resources through the business, but most family members do not have access to fortunes. Shares in the business are also frequently managed within trusts, not available to the beneficiaries as cash. These business-owning families therefore grow up in an upper-middle-class environment in which they may be taught to have purpose, work hard, participate in philanthropic behavior, and not be extravagant.

Then, change arrives in the form of a major liquidity event that unlocks the value embedded in the business, perhaps by selling the company or taking the company public. For the first time, the entire family now has real, liquid wealth as part of their lives. These Natives of moderate wealth now face change as turbulent as any first-generation stranger in paradise. An advantage is that many members already identify themselves with at least a moderate sense of growing up privileged. Still, they are faced with learning how to manage significantly more money in their personal lives than they ever had before. They also must take on the many responsibilities that come with wealth, including learning to adapt to their newfound identity as genuinely and personally wealthy. They must also deal with the disruption of losing the family business as the center of the family identity and purpose.

During the course of my career, I have seen client families of this type struggle surprisingly with this transition. Growing up with a successful family business, they believe they are prepared for having wealth directly in their hands. Many discover they are not as prepared as they

thought. Without the preparation, skill development, and family communication necessary to handle personal wealth, the family flounders
more than expected once the liquidity arrives. They don't realize the
degree to which they have been insulated from the stresses and responsibilities of personal wealth. Their long-awaited migration to significant wealth proves more disruptive than they imagined. These are the
families who thought they knew economic paradise well, only to discover they have more to learn than they realized.

When a Family Migrates Together

A large number of newcomers to wealth—like their ethnic immigrant
counterparts—migrate as a family. These are the members of a family
business, which is actually the most common and likely form of creating significant wealth. Family-run firms constitute over 80 percent of all
business enterprises in America and contribute to an estimated 70–90
percent of gross domestic product (GDP) globally.[29] Some of the most
successful companies in the world are owned and managed by multigenerational families whose wealth is intertwined with the business. This
includes a third of *Fortune 500* companies. Global families with famous
names, such as Hermès, Versace, and Louis Vuitton; industrial families,
such as the Walton, Mittal, Tata, or Quandt (of BMW) families; and
financial families, such as the Rothschilds or the Johnsons (of Fidelity
Investments), all draw the majority of their wealth from longstanding
family businesses. (The public knows some of the most prominent multigenerational family businesses through fiction better than they know
real families, for example, the Corleone Family in *The Godfather* trilogy.)

Families who create wealth together can do so in several ways. They
may be siblings operating as partners in a business. They may be parent
and adult child. Traditionally, a father and son might grow a company
that becomes the engine of the family's wealth. Now, father-daughter,
mother-daughter, and mother-son collaborations are increasingly common. In family businesses, Pioneers with strong-minded personalities
lead the journey toward success and the family's future. Others arrive
along the way, as they marry into the outpost being established or are
born into the family.

PLEASURES AND PERILS OF FAMILY MIGRATION

Families that migrate together experience the pleasures and perils of transitioning to wealth as a group. On one hand, they enjoy the benefits of close family support, shared decision-making, and the ability to evaluate risk through more than one set of eyes. Strong bonds within or between generations often hold the key to a family's success in leaving economic hardship behind.

The downsides of group migration can be just as powerful. With more members of the clan involved, squabbles over decisions and directions can derail the journey. Strong leadership and above-average capacity for collaboration are needed to sidestep potential rifts. The family must be able to navigate the complexities that are the hallmarks of family-run businesses: rivalries, arguments over whether to take risks, in-law issues, egos, differing business skills, entitlement, and a multitude of other pitfalls. All must be managed if the shared journey is to be successful.

And then, as mentioned above, the family must navigate the final turbocharged boost when the business is sold and family members come into real individual wealth. If the group maintains its sense of cohesion and adjusts to success in healthy ways, the family as a whole may adapt successfully. When family members choose markedly different strategies for coping with wealth, the risks to family harmony—and to the family itself—multiply. Given the high prevalence of family businesses in wealth creation, the shirtsleeves-to-shirtsleeves pattern is undoubtedly a function of the extra hazards of group migration to the Land of Wealth.

One Common Experience

One thing Immigrants and Natives alike must face is the complex cultural attitudes that exist between middle-class society and the wealthy. David Bork, a prominent family business consultant, captured society's deep ambivalence about wealth in commenting that, "in one culture after another, those without wealth seem to harbor a *hostile envy* directed toward those with wealth" [emphasis added].[30] Bork's phrase is echoed almost exactly by Dr. Suniya Luthar, a developmental psychologist who studies children growing up with affluence: ". . . [T]he rich are not only often the focus of envy and dislike . . . but are also aware that their misfortunes tend to evoke malicious pleasure in others."[31]

One of the unanticipated stresses faced by those migrating to wealth is contending with the transition from being on one side of these attitudes to the other. It is one thing to throw verbal stones at "The Rich" while living safely and securely among the comfort of your middle-class friends. It is altogether different when you become part of the group you once accused of being spoiled, entitled, self-centered, and ignorant of the real world. For Natives, hostile envy by others is a part of daily life and a part of identity. All inhabitants in the Land of Wealth must find ways to cope with society's complex attitudes toward them.

Generational Distinctions

Within the culture of wealth, abbreviated labels identify the first generation of wealth, the second, the third, and so on. It is more than a little ironic that these categories borrow terminology from the field of cross-cultural psychology and ethnic migration. Advisors and families have long been using the nomenclature of ethnic immigration without fully understanding the implications of these generational labels.

GENERATION ONE (G1)

Generation One, or G1, is the generation who makes the family's original migration to wealth, whether by the long slow Pioneer journey or the windfall Transplant experience. Their heritage culture is of the middle or working class, not wealth. When the question is asked about who originally brought the family anywhere into the Land of Wealth, the history book opens at G1.

G1s are typically well into adulthood when their transition to wealth occurs. Their adjustment to this transition therefore builds on a foundation of largely formed personality. The modern phenomenon of very young technology billionaires, exemplified by *Forbes 400* members Mark Zuckerberg and Dustin Moskovitz of Facebook, both in their mid- to late-twenties, is challenging this tradition. However, the most typical chronology of wealth creation spans the decades of life between G1s' forties and seventies, when their core of personality is already very well established.

GENERATION TWO (G2)

Those in Generation Two are the children of G1. Depending on their age at the time of the migration, they may have qualities that skew more towards Immigrant or more towards Native. Some G2s still retain memories of "when we lived in the old neighborhood," with its cramped kitchen, shared bathrooms, and tiny bedrooms. These older children (sometimes called "Generation 1.5" in the cross-cultural literature) grow up being admonished not to waste the toilet paper and to appreciate the few toys they received at holidays. In contrast, their younger brothers and sisters may have been toddlers during the economic journey, or perhaps they arrived on the scene after the family's outpost in the Land of Wealth was founded (which would make them Natives). They know only the new world of affluence, where living quarters and household budgets are much more expansive. Their experience of the family's heritage, and their connection to it, consists solely of stories their family tells them. To them, middle-class life was "Back Then." Affluent life is "Now" and, hopefully, "Forever." As much as their parents or grandparents may idealize the Old Country of economic adversity, the last thing these Natives want is to be sent back to where the family originally came from.

Cross-cultural psychology provides helpful age benchmarks for understanding children of immigrants.[32] Ethnic G2s who first encounter a new culture above the age of thirteen typically must adapt to their new environment in ways not unlike their immigrant parents. In contrast, G2s younger than five years old are largely influenced by the new culture, with little memory of where the family came from. Children between the ages of six and twelve may have mixed memories, experiences, and characteristics from the old and the new.

These benchmarks apply equally well for economic Immigrant families. Five-year-old children whose parents move up to more extravagant homes, transfer to more affluent school systems, and vacation in the Grand Caymans rather than the Grand Canyon will identify with the Land of Wealth as Natives. The same transition arriving in the life of a sixteen-year-old or a twenty-six-year-old G2 will impact a more fully formed personality. Birth order in G2 is not destiny. Nevertheless, it is a powerful influence in the creation of personality and identity.

Because of the simultaneous timelines of G2's individual development and their task of adjusting to the transition from one economic culture to another, G2 is often seen as a "bridge generation." They nest between their Immigrant parents in G1 and their likely more Native offspring in G3. G2s have a unique journey to navigate between the family's middle-class heritage and the family's adoptive culture of wealth. The journey of the family must cross the bridge generation of G2 if it is going to continue successfully to G3 and beyond.

GENERATION THREE (G3) AND BEYOND

G3s, G4s, and their offspring are the grandchildren and great-grandchildren of the original wealth-creating generation at G1. If the family's affluence has continued over time and the grandchildren primarily experience a life with wealth, G3s are fully Native. The Land of Wealth will remain their land of birth, whether or not they actually end up owning significant wealth themselves due to assets held in trust. Grandchildren born and raised with affluence may still harbor deep within themselves the legacy of the family's middle-class roots. But, as we shall see throughout this book, these residual elements must get blended into the family's new life through a successful process of adaptation.

The Journey Begins . . .

The Land of Wealth is far different than society's impression of a uniform mass of "The Rich." Economic paradise actually consists of a diverse multitude of highly individual Immigrants and a smaller group of equally unique Natives. Some inhabitants labored for years to enter, while others were swept up in an instant. A fortunate few share both Immigrant and Native qualities—familiar with the territory, yet experiencing the adventure of a new journey farther into the heights. What the Land of Wealth does not have is a large population of Natives born and bred with affluence, since all too often they have to leave paradise behind.

In the next Section, we'll move to understanding the next step for wealth's newcomers: adjusting to their new environment. How Immigrants choose to acculturate to wealth is extremely important on many levels. It will determine how they respond to the complexity that is the world of wealth. It will also influence how their families adapt to their new homeland, leading eventually either to healthy development of wealth's Natives or to the splintering and downfall of the family system.

II

Acculturation

CHAPTER 4

Adjusting to Paradise

All immigrants to foreign lands and cultures must leave behind the familiar to deal with new surroundings, new people, new rules, and new situations. The process of acculturation is rarely easy, though some individuals find the adjustment more straightforward than others do.

Immigrants to wealth are especially on their own in their newly discovered, sometimes bewildering economic paradise. Even with information overload about what to buy, where to live, what to drive, how to dress, and where to educate their children, there is precious little of substance to guide them on feeling comfortable and confident in their new paradise. Time and circumstance are also working against them. So, what are the most important factors that will determine how well or poorly they adjust? How can wealth's Immigrants successfully move past the first stages of survival and learn to thrive in their new homeland?

Understanding the Options for Acculturation

John W. Berry, Ph.D., a formulator of several core theories about cross-cultural psychology in ethnic groups, points out that, "When individuals and groups enter into an acculturation situation, they are faced with the questions: 'Who am I? To which group do I belong?'"[33] His words were echoed to me by Allan, a forty-nine-year-old entrepreneur who was raised in poverty and later sold his business for several hundred million dollars: "I don't know who I am anymore," Allan reported. "I live an entirely different life now, with people I never dreamed of being around. I just don't know how to be this new person."

Understanding wealth using a cultural lens allows us to benefit from decades of research in sociology and cross-cultural psychology to help answer these questions. According to theories on how immigrants resolve the natural dilemmas of acculturation, the options depend largely on two factors:

- The degree to which the immigrant chooses either to retain or let go of elements of the *heritage culture* he or she came from,

matched by

- The degree to which the immigrant either embraces or pushes away elements of the new *receiving culture* he or she has arrived in.[34]

Stated most simply, the primary questions wealth's Immigrants must answer are:

1. How much do I retain of the old culture?
2. How much do I take on of the new culture?
3. If I value and desire elements of both, how do I blend the various aspects to maximize the acculturation process, for me and for my family?

When we first formulated our metaphor about Immigrants and Natives to wealth, Dennis Jaffe and I called these questions "the Acquirers' Dilemmas."[35] Resolving these dilemmas forms the task each stranger in paradise must accomplish.

Figure 4-1 shows the options facing economic Immigrants as they, consciously or unconsciously, adapt to becoming wealthy. For simplicity, the following description will address the options from the standpoint of those who first come to wealth in the family. These options fully apply to that crucial first generation (G1) of Pioneering wealth-creators or windfall Transplants. Their adjustment is doubly important because it often helps establish the model for how others might adapt as well. The options also apply to the many other Immigrants who marry in at any generation.

Wealth's Immigrants arrive with a complex set of attitudes and behaviors rooted in their background. Their identity is closely tied to the economic culture of their birth. They have perspectives on relationships and speak the language of that culture. They approach money and wealth from the mindset of how they were raised.

In becoming wealthy, these Immigrants face whether and how to

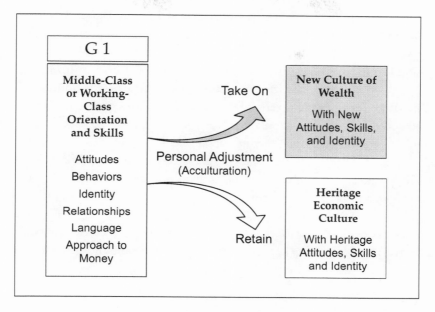

Figure 4-1: The options for adjusting to wealth

take on a new set of attitudes, skills, behaviors, language, and identity. Most arrive with little to no objective sense of what life will really be like in their adoptive land. They depend on their intuition, their values, and what they see around them to make early assessments about life in the culture of wealth. To make a successful adjustment to their new reality, what they really need is a roadmap.

Arriving in a Multicultural Land

The paradise encountered by wealth's Pioneers or Transplants is often far different than what they expected. Like immigrants to America from faraway countries, economic newcomers view wealth with an outsider's mentality. They rely on what they *believe* to be true about wealth, rather than what a positive adjustment to wealth really entails. These preconceived ideas, generally based upon TV, movies, books, and the opinions friends and family have about being rich, are frequently one-sided, inaccurate, or stereotypical.

For example, according to author and columnist David Brooks of *The New York Times*, "The Rich" are "Bourgeois Bohemians," or "Bobos," who are intelligent, educated, ambitious, and more liberal than their Old Money predecessors.[36] Robert Frank, a writer formerly at *The Wall Street Journal*, paints a different picture of what he calls the population of "Richistan." Frank asserts that the newly wealthy pursue happiness unsuccessfully while agonizing over the best means for everything: educating their children, buying yachts, decorating homes, or fulfilling dreams. He describes "Richistanis" using terms like superficial, excessively materialistic, and increasingly frenetic in their rise and fall.[37] Some strangers in paradise are more than happy to dive in and join the cultures these writers describe. Others believe they only have two choices: surrender completely to what sounds like a narcissistic culture, or cling bravely to a seemingly superior yet-not-quite-relevant middle-class culture. These are very limiting choices.

DIVERSITY OF PERSONALITIES

The migrations to affluence since the 1960s have changed what wealth is and how many subgroups exist within it. Modern studies of the affluent find clear subgroups with markedly different attitudes, behaviors, and approaches to being wealthy.[38] There may be somewhere between six and nine distinct subpopulations—consider them regions within the Land of Wealth—with dramatically different attitudes and behaviors toward materialism, philanthropy, desire for status, collaboration with advisors, and entrepreneurial orientation.[39] Notice the variety in the subgroups found by wealth industry experts Hannah Shaw Grove and Russ Alan Prince (Table 4-1).[40]

What is fascinating is that these subgroups correspond closely to money personality subtypes found to exist within the general population of the middle class.[41] This supports the concept that the wealthy arise from the middle class and migrate with many of their home culture's characteristics intact.

DIVERSITY OF GROUPS

Cross-cultural psychology discovered some time ago that acculturation does not operate in only one direction. Newcomers bring change of their own to their receiving cultures, especially in today's increasingly

Wealth Profile	Main Characteristic
Family Stewards	Focused on family, legacy, family business, and stewardship of wealth.
Independents	Focused on financial security and the independence it provides.
Accumulators	Save more than spend, live frugally, and disdain appearing wealthy.
The Anonymous	Cherish their privacy to an extreme, mistrusting most advisors.
Financial Phobics	Shy away from learning investing, preferring to delegate to advisors.
Innovators	Knowledgeable about investing and prefer cutting-edge ideas, products, and services.
Moguls	Motivated by power in business and in their families.
VIPs	Focused on prestige, status, and materialism.
Gamblers	Prefer the excitement of investing and chase performance.

Table 4-1: Nine personalities of the affluent, found in industry research. Abstracted from Hannah Shaw Grove and Russ Alan Prince, "The Psychology of Wealth," *Understanding the Wealthy*, Vol. 1, Issue 1 (2008).

complex world. As John W. Berry has written, ". . . while it used to be the case that . . . unicultural societies actually existed, it is now obvious that there is no contemporary society in which one culture, one language, one religion, and one single identity characterizes the whole population." [42] The same applies to the Land of Wealth.

In decades past, wealth was undoubtedly more of a melting pot, pressuring conformity toward norms that were predominantly white, male, elderly, conservative, Christian, and Anglo-Saxon. Reflecting the changing global culture, today's wealthy are increasingly female, younger, and racially and ethnically diverse, with a growing number of nontraditional households and sexual orientations.[43] With those who achieve wealth becoming more highly diverse, wealth itself has become a more plural, multicultural society.

This means that, contrary to popular belief, there is increasing latitude for newcomers and their offspring to craft individual identities, lifestyles, and values within wealth. They can find others of similar orientation and inclination, and they can provide mutual support to others trying to adapt to the new culture. Acculturation to wealth remains challenging, but at least wealth's Immigrants have broader choices to emulate or create.

———

Joan always made sure to arrive promptly for her group of successful female executives. They'd met once a quarter for years now, supporting each other through promotions, leadership challenges, and more than a few personal problems. It wasn't often Joan was in an all-female group of peers who cheered her success and helped her feel worthy of her executive position. They'd helped each other take important risks and had watched each other's salaries rise dramatically over time.

Tonight's conversation started with Joan's making a reference to her husband's veiled irritation to her earning more than he does. The room grew quiet as one after another acknowledged they avoid the topic with their husbands, too. The women shared with each other what they didn't feel comfortable sharing with male peers or female friends who weren't achieving business success. Several spoke about feeling like an imposter in the male-dominated executive world, while knowing in their heads that they deserved their place at the boardroom table. They offered empathy mixed with suggestions borne of experience and intelligence.

———

THE THREE MAIN STRATEGIES FOR ACCULTURATION

Cross-cultural psychology research, combined with the wealth psychology literature and lessons learned in consulting to wealthy families for several decades, points to three main coping strategies for how individuals can adjust to becoming wealthy.[44] These strategies involve whether to focus on holding onto one's heritage culture most tightly, embracing the new culture to the exclusion of the old, or blending the old and the new with varying degrees of balance.

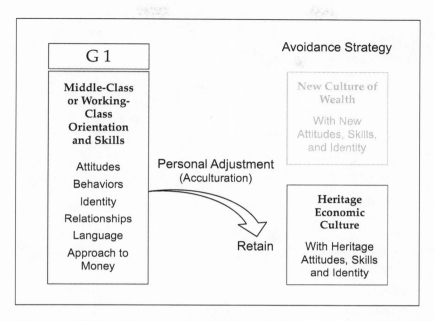

Figure 4-2: The acculturation strategy of Avoidance.

AVOIDANCE

Individuals using the coping strategy of Avoidance cling tightly to the culture of their heritage, avoiding or rejecting any transition toward the new culture they have entered (Figure 4-2).

With wealth, this strategy leads to a strong emphasis on retaining middle- or working-class attitudes, beliefs, and behaviors, adopting little of the alien and/or presumably toxic culture of affluence.[45] These individuals choose the perspective that "we are only middle class" so they can feel untainted by wealth and not surrender any of the values, attitudes, or behaviors they believe brought them to wealth.

ASSIMILATION

This approach is the opposite of Avoidance. With wealth, individuals adopting this strategy choose a headlong dive into acting "richer than The Rich" in their extravagant lifestyles. (Figure 4-3).

This strategy leads to abandoning the responsible values and behaviors learned in their heritage economic culture, in favor of embracing a

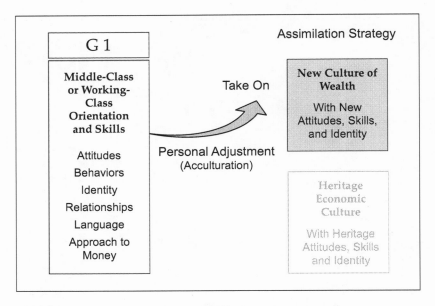

Figure 4-3: The acculturation strategy of Assimilation.

new culture focused on enjoying the lifestyle benefits of being wealthy. Assimilators may or may not adopt healthy attitudes about wealth. More frequently they adopt destructive attitudes and behaviors, at least in terms of a balanced approach to life and money.

INTEGRATION

The strategy of Integration combines elements from the home culture and the receiving culture to create an individual mosaic of adjustment, a kind of biculturalism (Figure 4-4).

Integration weaves together what works, comfortably, practically, and strategically for the individual. With wealth, this strategy attempts to create a workable mixture of the attitudes and behaviors from middle- or working-class roots alongside new attitudes and behaviors from an individual's present life with wealth. Integration is the more natural and healthy strategy for most economic Immigrants, as it is for most ethnic immigrants.

Integration offers the potential to achieve something even better:

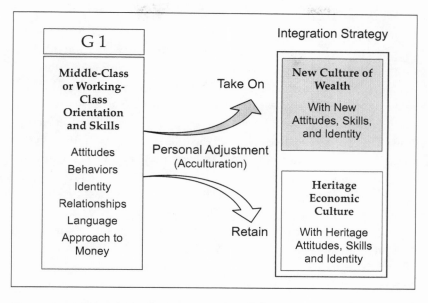

Figure 4-4: The acculturation strategy of Integration.

a "best of both worlds" approach that rises above simply weaving together elements from either culture. This higher-level perspective represents a deep understanding of the positive cores of middle-class culture and of affluence. It supports new attitudes and behaviors for living with wealth, including insights into how the family can adapt effectively to wealth across generations. Chapter 10 will expand on the elements seen in highly prosperous families using this deeper understanding.

The Failure to Adapt: Marginalization

Before exploring the three main strategies further, we must recognize one remaining strategy—termed *Marginalization*—that is the least successful strategy and has the poorest outcomes.[46] This is a somewhat rare and controversial subgroup in ethnic acculturation studies, where some immigrants struggle to make any adjustment whatsoever to their new circumstances. Benefiting little from either the past or the present, marginalized immigrants experience the unfortunate opposite of "the best of both worlds." Their experience becomes "the worst of both worlds."

Marginalization occurs when immigrants are unable or unwilling to retain much from their heritage culture, plus they fail to find a foothold in their adoptive land (sometimes due to being ostracized and excluded by their new neighbors). An example of marginalized ethnic immigrants might be an African family who flees the adversity of Somalia to settle in rural New England, only to find a much chillier reception than they anticipated. Not only would they find it difficult to live in their new surroundings, without support they would feel socially isolated and emotionally alone.

The cultural model of wealth would predict that, more often than we may know, some strangers in paradise also fail to achieve any level of adjustment. Failing to identify with their heritage roots or with wealth, these new citizens of the Land of Wealth wind up adrift without guidance by culture of any stripe. One example would be a working-class lottery winner who moves to an upscale neighborhood where he is shunned as an unwelcome interloper. Another would be a successful entrepreneur of color who finds little connection with either his country-club peers in a predominantly white suburb or with his extended family still living in an economically challenged urban environment.

Some experts in ethnic acculturation find only moderate support for the Marginalization profile compared to the other strategies.[47] The same may be true for wealth. I have not located any research or literature describing Marginalization among the wealthy, or if it exists, to what degree. In my years of wealth counseling, the only ones I have encountered are the occasional Transplants who marry into wealth and are never fully accepted by their new family, while also being emotionally abandoned by their family of origin.[48]

Interestingly, some Natives of wealth seem to lack effective strategies for coping with wealth and life, possibly representing a subgroup of marginalized adjusters in the second or third generation. Not feeling connected to the family's original middle-class roots or to their own cultural environment of wealth, these inheritors withdraw into a failure-to-thrive condition. It is primarily an identity issue, and unless they seek some sort of remedy, these individuals may forever remain the most estranged and marginalized citizens of paradise.

The Role of Learning and Experimentation

We shall explore each of the three main strategies of Avoidance, Assimilation, and Integration in depth throughout the remainder of this section. Keep in mind a key point. Immigrants typically experiment with adopting new cultural behaviors and shedding old ones in a gradual process over time, as they make their way eventually to an adjustment that fits. Choosing Avoidance, Assimilation, or Integration is not necessarily final—such as being forced to choose Door #1, Door #2, or Door #3 once and for all. Wealth's Immigrants may try on new behaviors and attitudes but not make these a permanent part of their identity right away. A newly affluent entrepreneur from the middle class may have to force himself many times to wear what he considers a pretentious and unnecessary tuxedo for a gala event. Yet eventually, tuxedos and galas may become comfortable parts of his new lifestyle and experiences.

Understandably, many newcomers to wealth begin by choosing the more black-and-white strategies of either Avoidance or Assimilation, launching them along a path that may seem like a smart decision in the short term. With time and accumulated experience, they may shift a little or a lot toward allowing some integration of their background with their new environment.

Figure 4-5 shows the broad spectrum of choices available to strangers in paradise as they to adjust to wealth.[49]

Think of this as a field containing clearly defined corners but much room to maneuver in between. One axis represents the degree to which an individual maintains his or her heritage economic culture and identity, from low (−) to high (+). The other axis represents the degree to which an individual accepts (and is accepted by) his or her new circumstances and culture of wealth, also from low to high.

Immigrants to wealth may be implementing strategies anywhere within this field. Over time, they may also shift in their approach, for example moderating their avoidance of wealth to move toward a greater acceptance of it in their perspectives, behaviors, and attitudes.

I know of no research in wealth that can tell us what proportions of the population stick with which strategy. Like the story of the six blind men trying to identify an elephant by feeling its various body parts,

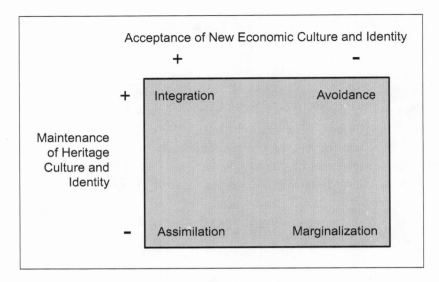

Figure 4-5: The spectrum of choices available for acculturation to wealth. Adapted from similar models delineated by John W. Berry, Ph.D., regarding ethnic acculturation.

guesses about how many Immigrants are in each subgroup probably depends on which aspects of wealth you see and touch yourself. Financial advisors and wealth consultants probably see representatives from all groups to varying degrees. However, as we shall discover, those in the Avoidance group may keep themselves hidden and therefore seem under-represented in the culture of wealth. But they are there.

Exploring the Three Strategies of Acculturation

Arriving in economic paradise is not the end-point envisioned by wealth's Immigrants. It actually begins the real work of adjusting to a new culture in all its complexities. In the following chapters, we'll explore the main coping strategies facing those fortunate enough to migrate to wealth—Avoidance, Assimilation, and Integration.

Do not forget, however, the age-old warning about shirtsleeves-to-shirtsleeves. The stakes are high and the clock is ticking as newcomers start down their paths of adjustment. Each strategy is an option for the Immigrant on his own, *if* he wants to remain in paradise. But one path offers something more: the opportunity for future generations to stay.

CHAPTER 5

Avoidance:
"We Are Only Middle Class"

In the film adaptation of the play *Driving Miss Daisy,*[50] Daisy Werthan is a wealthy first-generation matriarch who is clearly not very happy in paradise. Her deceased husband and her grown son have built a successful business that transported the family to a world of affluence. Miss Daisy adamantly refuses to accept the trappings of wealth.

Due to some driving mishaps, Daisy is forced to accept a chauffeur, despite her resistance to the idea. When Hoke, her chauffeur, picks her up one day in front of her friends, Daisy burns with embarrassment. She scolds him, saying, "I could see what they were thinking when we came out." Which, in her view, is that they thought she "was pretending to be rich." Hoke points out reality: "You IS rich," to which she retorts, "No I'm not! . . . On Forsyth Street [her old neighborhood] we made many meals out of grits and gravy. I have done without, plenty of times." Daisy also notices when a 33-cent can of salmon goes missing. She refuses to use the air conditioning in her car despite the Southern heat. She turns up her nose at the extravagances of her daughter-in-law who seems only too happy to assimilate into high society and wealth.

Over the course of twenty-five years, Daisy continues to live by the rules, attitudes, and identity of her middle-class culture. She makes only the most gradual concessions to the world of wealth around her.

How Avoidance Manifests in the Land of Wealth

Whether from Madagascar or Mexico, China or Chile, Ireland or Indonesia, some immigrant families in America choose to preserve the beloved aspects of their home culture as much as possible. From the

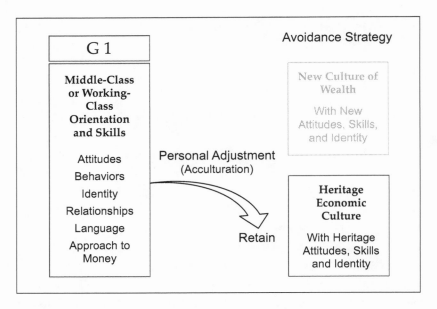

Figure 5-1: The acculturation strategy of Avoidance

books on their shelves to the paintings on their walls, the food on their table, and the lullabies they sing to their children at night, they cling tightly to their cultural heritage. Some choose Avoidance because they feel most comfortable living as if still in the Old Country. Some fear that surrendering—or even loosening their grip on—their beloved values and traditions will corrupt rather than empower them. Even though they migrated to take advantage of America's opportunities and security, they avoid embracing any changes in lifestyle or beliefs offered by the new environment.

Economic Immigrants are susceptible to the same strategy of Avoidance (Figure 5-1). They decide wealth has more negatives than positives and that they prefer not to "fit in." It just isn't for them—and certainly not for their children. They choose Avoidance, a kind of denial of wealth, and identify themselves forevermore as "middle-class people who happen to have a lot of money."

Even if they choose to trade up to a bit more affluent home, Avoiders don't alter the habits and attitudes of their middle-class roots. They shun the trappings of wealth, continuing to live their lives undisturbed by whatever their windfall or success has achieved—and what it could provide. Their bank accounts have grown—perhaps quite significantly —but they choose to remain unchanged by the event.

This approach pushes away the reality of the family's financial success in favor of preserving the appearance and identity of their middle-class homeland. In doing so, it keeps away the many benefits a more balanced approach would provide, such as learning how to manage their wealth for the long term, teaching their children financial skills, or providing for their children educational opportunities the G1s would never have had.

———

As Joan and Ted talked over what to do about their incredible windfall, two things were certain. One was that they would not signal to anyone that they now were wealthy. Ted, in particular, was adamant that advisors couldn't be trusted, that scam artists would target them, and that they would be pressured to make loans and provide gifts to friends and family who should be responsible for their own lives. He did not want the hassle of dealing with any of that. He was perfectly happy living the way he did. He disliked rich people and didn't want to be seen as one of them.

The other decision was that informing even their children would be, in their view, a disaster. Joan and Ted committed themselves to insulating their kids as long as possible from what they saw as the contamination that comes from having too much money. They were willing to take on the risk, and the responsibility, of hiding the family's fortune from their children, even though this meant their children would likely miss out on many opportunities. They believed they were being caring parents.

———

NOT JUST THE MILLIONAIRE NEXT DOOR

The strategy of Avoidance is more extreme than simply being what is often referred to as the "millionaire next door,"[51] characterized as having assets totaling several million dollars yet choosing to drive the proverbial ten-year-old Toyota, live in an upscale but not extravagant house, send their kids to public schools, and continue coaching Little

League. It is a more severe denial of being wealthy, as well as a desire to preserve anonymity, much like the Anonymous subtype found in the research by Grove and Prince mentioned in Chapter 3.

Avoidance also isn't reflected in the life choices billionaires like Warren Buffett make. While possessing vast wealth, Buffett continues to maintain many of his middle-class habits, yet he has evidently adjusted to the massive growth of his fortune over his lifetime. When necessary or advisable, he uses private jets and luxury accommodations. He publicly associates with others of similar wealth and, most importantly, he appears comfortable with his identity as one of the richest men in the world. That is not coping by avoiding wealth. That is someone using the Integration approach, which we'll discuss in Chapter 7.

Motivations for Choosing Avoidance

Some Immigrants who choose Avoidance have healthy or understandable motivations. It's the hidden motivations that cause problems.

For many, Avoidance is an initial response to the fear that crucial aspects of themselves, and the values that brought them to wealth, will be lost if they adopt a wealthy lifestyle. Their desire to preserve their lives in a middle-class bubble shares many of the motivations ethnic immigrants hold in the same circumstances. Both tend, for example, to idealize their heritage culture while exaggerating or misconstruing what they view as the receiving culture's negative aspects. For economic Immigrants, this translates to extolling the virtues of middle-class life —supposedly the sole province of hard work, perseverance, self-sufficiency, grounded values, and family harmony—while denigrating the culture of wealth as uniformly shallow, materialistic, valueless, purposeless, and power-hungry. They believe that appearing to be anything more than middle class will attract only the worst sort of attention.

The choice to bar wealth from the home, as if it were a charming but predatory guest, grows from accepting the profoundly negative stereotypes perpetuated about the wealthy. These Avoiders fall sway to a sort of blind acceptance that "The Rich" are a species that must be avoided, unless the Immigrants wish to be corrupted. Avoiders are seduced by black-or-white thinking, viewing their heritage middle-class life as uniformly rosy and their new wealthy status as completely toxic. They are wrong on both counts.

By rationalizing the Old Country of middle class life as all good and the new Land of Wealth as all bad, those Immigrants choosing Avoidance are able to remain in their comfort zone. They don't have to alter their identity, their behavior, or their attitudes. They answer those two questions of acculturation (who am I? what group do I belong to?) with simplicity: "I am middle class, now and forever."

THEY FEAR THE LOSS OF COMMUNITY

Another motivation for choosing Avoidance is the belief or reality that embracing wealth will lead to the loss of precious ties to others. The bonds of old relationships and sense of community may be more highly valued than any desire to create new ones. For some, Avoidance may feel like a necessary stance in preserving original, pre-wealth ties to people who may not be able to accept even a partial sharing of the Immigrant with a new culture.

This is particularly an issue for women and people of color. Ethnic, racial, and religious communities are less commonly wealthy, which means their powerful social bonds may be based in part on the *shared experience* of economic vulnerability. Oppression and exclusion by economically privileged groups may have created deep divisions that can influence a community's response to a member's sudden wealth.

For these minority wealth holders, ties to their personal communities may hold far more importance than their desire to affiliate with people who have harmed their communities in the past or present. Unaware of or unable to find subcultures that resemble theirs in the Land of Wealth, they prefer to maintain their dedication to their heritage communities. This is quite different from an inability to adapt to wealth. It reflects the tension inherent in trying to bridge two historically conflicted worlds.

Avoidance may also be chosen to ward off being rejected by the new community of wealth. Some less-traditional newcomers to wealth (women, people of color, people from working-class backgrounds) have experienced wealth as a social dividing line—a club that reserves membership solely for white males. Wealth holders from diverse backgrounds may anticipate prospective problems with acceptance and choose not to present themselves to find out how welcome or unwelcome they might be. They prefer choosing Avoidance to minimize the more dire circumstance of becoming marginalized, isolated, and alone.

THEY HAVE MORAL REASONS FOR RESISTING WEALTH

Others choose this strategy for philosophical, religious, or political reasons. Some of wealth's citizens have strong views about wealth inequality or the purpose of money in society, as in the oft-cited New Testament quotation: "It is easier for a camel to go through the eye of a needle than for a rich man to enter the kingdom of God." They may share strongly liberal or socially progressive views that disparities in wealth distribution harm the most vulnerable members of society and should not persist.

These Immigrants to wealth then follow the self-effacing path exemplified by inheritors such as Christopher Mogil and Ann (Slepian) Ellinger, who co-wrote *We Gave Away a Fortune*.[52] This use of wealth for social rather than personal benefit is rooted in well-articulated philosophies instead of emotional issues about coping with becoming or being wealthy. This group takes a highly altruistic approach, often deciding to decline or give away most of their money in favor of remaining part of the middle-class majority.

Again, however, the position of these citizens of paradise is more extreme than the stance of wealth-holders who make outsized philanthropy a central part of their estate planning. The Billionaire Giving Pledge, championed by Bill Gates, Warren Buffett, and others, encourages highly successful entrepreneurs to donate a majority of their fortunes to charitable purposes, during their lifetimes or after death. This still leaves very sizable fortunes for the family to enjoy or for other purposes. Philanthropy this generous can honor the values of the entrepreneur's heritage culture while also embracing the social responsibility often associated with wealth. This reflects Integration, not Avoidance.

THEY NEED A SHORT-TERM STRATEGY

Many of wealth's newer Immigrants sort through these motivations, philosophies, and trade-offs as they decide what to do with their new situation. For them, Avoidance serves as a postponement strategy. It is like sitting by the side of the lake, reluctant to enter what looks like very cold water, until they feel ready to wade into their new environment. Avoidance need not be a permanent refusal to bridge old and new worlds. It may be chosen as a preliminary position to be gradually relinquished over time, as the strangeness of paradise wears off.

For others, Avoidance is a stance they plan to maintain indefinitely. They simply do not want to adapt.

The Fearful Frugal

———

When the money finally arrived from SteriMetrix's sale, Joan and Ted didn't need to talk much about where or how to invest it. Joan just transferred it into the accounts they already had, either at banks in town or in an online brokerage account. She tried to avoid thinking about it. It was as if her skills as a CFO were part of another world, not touching her life at home.

Any potential investment growth begged the question: why? They now had more money than they would ever use anyway. Their personal financial management was driven mostly by caution, extreme privacy, and an overemphasis on security, especially by Ted. As a result, Joan and Ted never used their financial assets to make reasonable purchases that could have improved their lives—a much better car for Joan, a larger house, and some much-needed vacation time in relaxing locales. Every time they considered spending some of their SteriMetrix money, one or the other backed away. Better to hoard the money and avoid exposure, they thought, even if it meant living a life of self-imposed hardship.

———

BY THEIR VERY NATURE, STRANGERS IN PARADISE WHO AVOID SPENDing or investing their wealth tend to remain hidden. They can go unnoticed until their estate gets revealed after death, or relatives discover what has been going on, or someone in the next generation reveals their family secret. Such was the case of LeRoy Beckman of Montana, who bought hearing aids at secondhand stores, heated only one room in his house, drove an old panel truck, and died at age eighty-eight leaving an estate of nearly $3 million.[53] Or the frugal, unassuming California man who surprised his family by leaving a stunning $100 million estate, accumulated from an equity position in a private company where he was employed.[54]

Those we might call The Fearful Frugal are marked by the large disconnect between their wealth and their spending habits. Like Miss Daisy, they find it hard to leave behind some or all of the following beliefs:

- Disaster lies around the next corner.
- Be as frugal as you can, to a fault.
- Avoid all signs of "flashiness."
- Reuse whatever you can until all usefulness has been squeezed out.
- Get the lowest price for everything, no matter how trivial.
- Don't trust anyone (especially advisors) unless they share your views about money, and even then, tell them only the minimum they need to know.
- If people find out you have money, they will try to take advantage of you.

The Fearful Frugal may occasionally purchase something grand yet always with an eye to whether a) it is a good investment, b) they can get it at a bargain, or c) it provides quality for the price. Examples include the Scrooge-like business owner who buys a Cadillac or Mercedes but oversees meetings in twenty-year-old suits that "still have some life left in them." Or his dowager wife who drains shampoo leftovers into one bottle for the guestroom shower "because things shouldn't go to waste."

These Avoiders continue to take an exclusively bottom-up approach to any purchase. They view expenditures from a middle-class perspective ("how much will this cost me?") rather than a more nuanced approach that evaluates purchases intelligently from multiple perspectives ("Can I afford it without damaging my finances? Will this save me time? Have I made other large purchases lately which mean I should delay this one?").

The Perils of Avoidance

Some of the wealthy and many of their advisors think the attitudes described above are admirable. As one advisor said to me regarding such a client, "What's wrong with that? It sounds like they are being good stewards of their wealth to me. If more of the wealthy took that approach, they'd have a lot more money and a lot less heartache."

Prudence with money is not wrong—far from it. The problem is that this level of penny-pinching is grounded in anxiety and mistrust that never go away, despite plenty of long-term financial security and stability. These money habits were prudent in the *prior* era of middle-class life, no longer relevant to current circumstances. Harvesting shampoo dregs or dressing in well-worn suits has a miniscule impact on long-term wealth at the $10 million or $50 million level. Investment asset allocation, portfolio management, or major purchases such as homes are the real decisions impacting the growth or maintenance of wealth.

The damage done by maintaining a perspective of extreme frugality is immense and sad. These individuals can never truly relax. Not only do they scrutinize every purchase for its emphasis on value, every purchase made by others is equally judged. Vigilance and mistrust rule the day.

How Avoidance Impacts the Children

The long-term problems for those avoiding any acculturation to wealth are similar to what ethnic immigrants face when they create a world-within-a-world environment: They don't permit the benefits of the new culture to help their children's lives, and they aren't preparing their children to live in the culture that may someday be part of their children's lives.

———

When their older children were ready for college (prior to the sale of SteriMetrix), Ted and Joan insisted they apply only to public colleges and universities, even though the family had already saved more than enough to be considered upper-middle-class. They felt private institutions were just not worth the money. There was some stickiness around filling out financial aid forms due to the necessity to disclose the family's resources. Ted and Joan were faced with either lying on the forms or coming up with some explanation to their children about why needs-based financial aid was not going to be possible.

Their solution was to say they had been scrimping and saving for college education since their children were little. The rationale that money had to be put away for college provided cover many times for why the family would not pay for various "luxuries." Joan and Ted also required that their older kids take out student loans to supplement the family's payments for tuition, just so their children would bear some of the burden for the cost of college and have to pay back loans afterwards.

They did the same when their youngest son Sam started applying to college, even though their post-liquidity finances could now easily support the full range of colleges and universities. One of his first choices was a nearby private university with a strong department in his major area of interest. Ted and Joan scoffed at the expensive tuition and refused to consider it. Years later, circumstances would reveal to Sam his parents' subterfuges in this and many other ways, significantly damaging their relationship.

———

G1's NEGATIVE ATTITUDE TOWARD WEALTH CAN HAVE AN IMPACT far beyond their generation. Their fears often lead to over-controlling behaviors, believing that children must be monitored closely to eradicate any inclination to spend frivolously. Harsh money messages of fear and wastefulness must be drummed in to indoctrinate the next generation to their parents' frugal ways. One result is that inheritors develop highly negative attitudes about money and are rarely taught about personal financial management in a broad, balanced way. Fear and money are bundled together tightly and passed on as one inheritance.

THEY END UP DEPORTED

Parents who refuse to create a suitably affluent home, despite the capacity to do so, usually see themselves as wise, selfless, and restrained. They'll say, "We just want our kids to be normal," benchmarking "normal" as the middle-class life they had grown up in.[55] The problem is that these parents have never seen a roadmap showing successful parenting with wealth. They believe, incorrectly, that such a journey inevitably leads to crashes. So they navigate by the only guidebook they know—the middle-class way.

Some parents, at more modest levels of wealth, do the math and conclude there's no reason to prepare their children for wealth. Distribution of $5 million or $10 million among four kids, after taxes and the parents' own need for retirement assets, may well lead their children back to an upper-middle-class life but not wealth. This is realistic. But what these well-meaning parents miss is that, to whatever extent the children are exposed to affluence growing up, they will still need skills for good financial self-management and for understanding the world from an upper-middle-class perspective, rather than their parents' heritage middle-class perspective.

At heart, parents' real motivation may not be so altruistic as they would like to believe. They possess such a strong middle-class perspective that living any other way would literally feel foreign. They *like* defining themselves as middle-class people, with middle-class habits, friends, history, food, and recreational activities. They aren't just preserving the home as a haven of middle-class life for their kids. They're preserving it for themselves.

THEY LEARN DISTORTED VALUES

Years ago, I drove into a New York City suburb to meet Neil, a young man seeking help to overcome his constant stress about money. Although he had not yet told me the level of his family's wealth, I suspected it was considerable.

While planning the logistics of meeting him, I mentioned I would park my car in the public garage next to his office and walk over. Neil said, "Oh, don't do that. The parking garage fee is exorbitant! I'll get you a parking spot on a street nearby, and you can just feed the meter." He insisted we go through an elaborate routine where he held a parking space with his car on a side street several blocks away for me.

On my drive in, we exchanged phone calls several times until I found him and pulled into the tight space he vacated between two hulking SUVs. I dug up barely enough coins for two hours on the meter. As I walked in the rain toward his building, through a maze of streets, I got lost. More texting and calls later, I finally arrived, nearly a half-hour late and a bit damp. Throughout our subsequent meeting, weighing on my mind were thoughts about whether my car would be crunched by one of those SUVs as they left, or whether I might get a parking ticket if our meeting ran over the time on the meter.

During our conversation, Neil opened up about how money anxiety invaded his romantic attachments, his ability to decide on jobs, and his complicated relationship with his highly frugal parents. He had learned some years back that his parents had built a net worth of approximately $70 million from his father's investment banking career. Yet they scrutinized each purchase as if their survival depended on it. Neil's father also handled most home improvement and financial tasks because he didn't trust anyone to do them.

Because Neil acted nearly as frugally as his parents, they had begun to shift some of their wealth into his hands. Neil sensed his own attitudes about money were distorted in some way, but he couldn't imagine any approach that might be more reasonable.

I decided to use the events of that morning as a teachable moment. I pointed out that, in Neil's insistence that I pay a few dollars to a parking meter instead of $30 to a parking garage, we'd lost nearly half an hour of our limited meeting time, I risked a parking ticket, and I could sustain possible damage to my car. At the very least, we had both gone through unnecessary stress. Because we each could easily afford the parking garage fee, his desire to have me engage in "prudent" spending had actually backfired.

That morning was the beginning of a new, more balanced perspective for Neil. He realized two things for the first time. One was how much his parents' attitudes about money had invaded his judgment. He had been more interested in saving $26 than in maximizing our time together or considering my comfort and convenience. The second was how he in turn brought the distorted behaviors of his family to his relationships. He had fully expected I would admire his ingenuity in saving a few dollars, when in fact it seemed he was putting money ahead of our more pressing mutual needs.

Neil gradually learned which values from his parents' middle-class upbringing he wanted to consciously retain and which could be discarded as too narrow or outmoded for his present life. He also learned to make decisions more appropriate to the world of wealth he now had access to and which he someday would manage.

THEY LIVE IN A CULTURE OF LIES

Generation One parents who choose to hide their affluence withhold more than their money from their children. They also withhold the truth, choosing to lie by commission or by omission about the family's economic circumstances.

Several years after SteriMetrix's sale, Joan and her sister Caroline strolled, sandals in hand, along the white sand beach on Florida's Gulf Coast, catching up on family news. Joan's family, friends, and children were all aware of the event, but only Caroline knew Joan had been a partner and had shared in the windfall.

When Caroline inquired how Joan's children were handling the family's newfound fortune, Joan smiled thinly and said, "Oh, Ted and I decided not to tell them I was a partner in the company. We told Rachel and the boys we had gotten a bit of a windfall when the company was sold but that we lost a lot of it when the market turned down a while back. That way, they wouldn't think we—or they—are rich. We want them to just be regular kids. We figure we'll tell them someday when they can handle it." Caroline was so stunned she stopped short and gaped at her sister. All she could think about was the precious time and opportunity Joan was wasting, plus what would happen if the kids ever found out.

How Avoidance Impacts Estate Planning

There comes a point when Avoidance must end. Despite their ingrained refusal to embrace their wealth, Avoiders approaching the end of their lives must decide what to do with the fortune they somehow accumulated. They have to address the dilemmas of disclosure and distribution of wealth through various estate-planning options, none of which are ideal.

THEY LET THE CHIPS FALL WHERE THEY MAY

Some Avoiders procrastinate about dealing with estate planning until it is too late. They remain paralyzed by the habit of avoidance or by the unhappy options facing them. The family is then left to deal with the fallout: a drawn-out probate process, unnecessary tax bills, and, importantly, the disclosure of the wealth itself.

When grown children finally discover that their parents hid the facts about the family's wealth, reactions can vary widely. Sometimes the best happens. Some children appreciate that the desire to protect them was done in the interest of creating strong values and healthy personalities. They may believe, as their parents did, that disclosure about wealth is inherently demotivating, that it will foster greed and lead to children pestering parents to spread the money around. Warnings from advisors and real-life horror stories about grasping, lazy inheritors pressuring their parents often fuel these fears.

However, adult children can also react with shock when they first learn about the family's wealth. This is not because they are spoiled or feel entitled, but because they have been lied to about a key aspect of the family. What their parents viewed as rightfully private was actually important information relevant to the relationships, planning, and identity of everyone in the family.[56]

I've counseled many G2 clients who struggled to make sense of the news that their parents were wealthy, usually without being able to ask their now-deceased parents why they chose to handle things this way in the life of the family. I've also worked with families in estate-planning meetings where the disclosure occurred during discussion with the parents themselves. Natural questions, awkward to voice out of fear of appearing ungrateful, were raised by the next generation, such as: "Why couldn't you trust us enough to tell us the truth?" or "What else have you not told us?" Adult children who thought they were trusted or that the family operated honestly may be understandably dismayed at being insulated for years, without their awareness or permission.[57]

The next generation may also react to what they now see as lost opportunities. Many G2s wish they could have shown their parents how *well* they handled the money, not how poorly. They were denied seeing their parents be proud of them, because their parents were more afraid of being disappointed in them.

Worse yet, what highly frugal parents view as "healthy growth experiences that teach the value of a dollar" can feel infuriating to adult children forced to make hard choices that permanently limited opportunity, growth, or independence. This is particularly true if limited financial resources kept the children tied to unhealthy situations, such as dead-end jobs, dangerous neighborhoods, or abusive relationships.

As a method of handling the risks of communicating about wealth in families, "don't tell the kids anything, ever" is a page drawn from middle-class ideas about the Land of Wealth. Lack of motivation, entitlement, and pressure to spend irresponsibly can be managed if parents know what to do and when to do it. These risks are more easily handled when open communication starts at an early age, the opposite of what most families think. Section III will address various methods used in wealthy families to teach responsibility and offset entitlement in family members.

The net result of Avoiders leaving no guidance for their offspring is that the next generation starts its own journey to wealth in shock. They become Transplants whose inheritance suddenly jolts them out of middle-class life. They must then learn to acculturate to their new financial circumstances in whatever way they can, with few good models to follow.

THEY GIVE IT AWAY

Some Avoiders decide to donate their entire fortune to philanthropic causes rather than pass it on in the family. They remain adamant—right to the end—that wealth is truly toxic or that it should not be foisted upon anyone who has not earned it himself or herself. They believe that Pioneering Immigrants are the only ones who should have access to paradise. As such, instead of granting passports to wealth for their own children via inheritance, they give away the money. Yes, G1s have every right to do what they want with their money. But this solution is often driven more by fear of doing damage than by making educated choices among all the possible alternatives.

It is important to note here that some families of faith feel very strongly that they are temporary stewards of wealth that truly belongs to God. For these families, passing the wealth completely to their family may feel like a betrayal of that stewardship. This has little to do with how the wealth-creating generation is choosing to cope with their economic cultural transition. It has more to do with the principles and values of how they view money as part of their faith and life. They are not avoiding adaptation to wealth. They are making conscious choices to put their values ahead of their children's rights or abilities to be wealthy.

THEY PASS IT ON TOO LATE TO DO MUCH GOOD

Some Avoiders delay wealth transfers as long as possible, bequeathing their wealth exclusively through second-to-die plans which bequeath the fortune first to the surviving spouse, then to adult children when the spouse passes on. Given the longevity of elders these days, those adult children may easily be in their sixties before they are faced with the challenges associated with managing wealth. G1s choose this option in hopes that G2s won't be able to do much damage—but it also means they don't have opportunities to do much good either. In choosing this option, Avoiders are betting that children raised in a middle-class life, with middle-class values, will make solid financial decisions with whatever money they receive.

The risk, however, is that their children will be unprepared to handle an influx of significantly larger amounts of money than what they've been earning on their own. A middle-class upbringing is no guarantee of healthy development or good skills with wealth, particularly in a family with a history of not discussing money, negative attitudes toward "The Rich," deep mistrust of advisors, and no training for the decisions and responsibilities that come with wealth. These new strangers in paradise must now make their own best guesses, unprepared as they may be to do so.

My experience is that G2s who inherit unexpected wealth from Avoiders often wind up struggling with anxiety, guilt, or bitter rebellion. Each spending decision must be scrutinized through two lenses: the middle-class view and the wealth view. Both are distorted for these inheritors. When your net worth is now in the millions yet you can still hear your parents' critical voices in your head, it's hard to make rational decisions about the value of a moderately expensive meal ("These prices are ridiculous!"), a cab ride ("You could always walk, it's not that far."), or a bathroom renovation ("You don't need such fancy lights, it's only a bathroom."). Some G2s solve this by drowning out the parental voice and spending without limits, seeking whatever pleasures affluence can bring. They fall prey to the equally damaging strategy of Assimilation, discussed in the next chapter. Others are sentenced to living perpetually with a strained relationship to the money.

THEY LOCK IT UP IN TRUST

A common option "we are only middle class" Avoiders choose is to pass on the money via tightly controlled trusts that perpetuate G1's control from the grave. This method enshrines G1's mistrust and protectionism of children by placing all management of the money in trustees' hands.

Overly controlling parents who never adjusted to their own wealth tend to designate strict conditions for how trustees dole out income or principal. They designate advanced age benchmarks for when trust principal may be distributed: ages fifty, fifty-five, and sixty, for example, rather than younger benchmarks of thirty, forty, and forty-five. G1 Avoiders also seem to like incentive provisions that legislate behavior. In a vicious cycle, they feel they need to do so because they view their children as untrained about wealth and at risk for mismanaging any fortune that may wind up in their hands. The fact that the parents never prepared the children for any inheritance gets forgotten.

As may be expected, the dysfunctional family dynamics around money get replayed again and again between the beneficiaries of these highly controlling trusts and the trustees who serve in the stead of the parents.

————

Joan was growing tired of hiding their wealth as completely as Ted wanted. But he overruled her whenever the issue came up. The strains in the marriage widened when Joan pushed Ted to address estate planning after his minor heart attack at age sixty-two.

They went to see a lawyer to create a basic will. When the lawyer asked if they had any significant assets they might want to protect for the next generation, they had to say yes. They refused to disclose any specifics to this attorney, of course, only that they wanted to preserve what they had worked hard to build.

What appalled Joan was how much Ted wanted to exert control over the money long after he was gone. He pushed for creating trusts with strict provisions about what the money could be used for—even for Joan —saying he didn't want her tempted to change her lifestyle. He wanted income for the children to be delayed and sharply limited, with portions of principal to be distributed after they were well into their fifties. The money could only be used for retirement backup when the children were older or for strictly defined educational support for any grandchildren. He also wanted to make their middle son a trustee over the other children, even though Ted Junior had no experience in these matters and was seen as cold-hearted by the others.

Joan went along with Ted's instructions, but she had grave misgivings. She could not shake the feeling these plans would destroy the family.

———

The Challenges of Avoidance

Using the acculturation strategy of Avoidance, some strangers in paradise choose to retain the identity and attitudes of their economic upbringing as much and as long as possible. They believe this is the best option for the family to remain in the familiar—and, in their viewpoint, superior—culture of middle-class life, with the bonus of having plenty of money as backup. Underneath this strategy, however, lie deep struggles about navigating relationships, social connections, identity, and behavior. Some simply choose to stay with what they know. For others, the strategy of Avoidance is based on fear, stereotyping, and mistrust.

More importantly, the failure to provide guidance for the next generation ultimately creates a different set of problems. By refusing to face wealth or prepare their children for handling it, these "We are only middle class, now and forever" Immigrants leave the next generation ill-prepared for maintaining the wealth that may have been so hard to accumulate. These G1s bring on the very damage they associate with wealth—that it either corrupts succeeding generations or leaves them guilt-ridden, anxious, and unhappy. The children of Avoiders might learn about money from their parents, but they will not learn about wealth.

There are better strategies that promote a balance between the past and the present. But first we must understand the polar opposite of Avoidance, an equally shortsighted approach to the challenges of acculturation called Assimilation.

CHAPTER 6

Assimilation: "We Will Be Richer than 'The Rich'"

If we were to believe what movies and novels tell us, nearly everyone who becomes wealthy falls prey to the approach called Assimilation. It is what society imagines is inevitable when the frailty of human nature responds to the siren call of wealth.

An extreme example is Jay Gatsby, the leading character in F. Scott Fitzgerald's *The Great Gatsby*. Gatsby seems to have it all: great wealth, an exuberant social life, smooth charm, and many admirers. He promotes the impression he came from wealth, and in his business dealings he seeks to enhance his fortune as much as he can. Gatsby actually arose from poverty, a circumstance he tries to hide until he is discovered. He had transformed himself from James Gatz, a poor North Dakotan, to Jay Gatsby, supposedly a member of moneyed gentry who was educated at Oxford and lives a life of leisure.

A more contemporary example is Bud Fox, the young stockbroker in the movie *Wall Street*[58] who gets drawn into the world of the successful and amoral Gordon Gekko (the notorious advocate of the phrase "greed is good"). As Bud rises in the investment world, he leaves behind the positive values his father taught him in middle-class life: Maintain a strong work ethic, be mindful of responsible spending and saving, enjoy the fruits of your labor, avoid unnecessary extravagance, think of your fellow man.

Both Jay Gatsby and Bud Fox personify the negatives that society attributes to the wealthy: shallowness, dubious ethics, self-gratification, and lack of purpose. In the end, their worlds are unsustainable, and each ends tragically.

How Assimilation Manifests in the Land of Wealth

Ethnic immigrants who choose assimilation strive to blend in as completely as they can to their new American homeland. They try to scrub their speech of any foreign accent. They take on new clothes, music, behaviors, and attitudes. Success in assimilation is measured by the degree to which the immigrant can "pass" as an American outwardly and think like an American inwardly.

Assimilation (Figure 6-1) has its inherent limitations in acculturating to a new environment. Ethnic immigrants may assimilate into their *image* of what America is, not necessarily to the full complexity of American culture itself. They may wind up taking on a stereotype of being American, which doesn't reflect how many true Americans act or believe. The upside is the benefit of fitting in and adjusting quickly. The downside is that many ethnic assimilators also wind up losing the beneficial legacy of their family's heritage. The Old Country helped form the character, identity, values, and history for the immigrant and his or her family. Even if they wish to abandon them, the family's cultural roots are still the foundation for the present and the future.

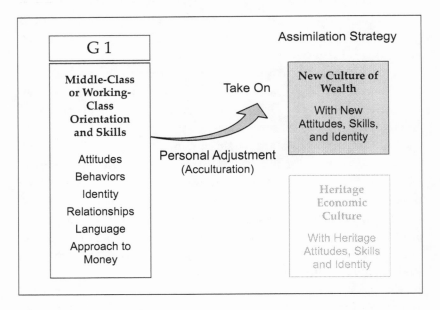

Figure 6-1: The acculturation strategy of Assimilation.

Some economic Immigrants take the same approach. They eagerly shed all traces of their middle-class heritage to adopt a new identity as a person of wealth. Instead of hesitating lakeside, debating whether to dip a toe into unfamiliar and potentially dangerous waters, these Immigrants dive right in. They seem driven by a desire to cleanse themselves of where they came from. They aspire to act "richer than The Rich."

Like Avoiders, the strategy of Assimilation embraces the *image* of what wealth seems to be from an outsiders' perspective, not the reality of wealth in its full complexity. Unlike Avoiders who think wealth is terrible, Assimilators view wealth as glorious. There is certainly no shortage of images to draw from. Besides the portrayals of "The Rich" in movies, plays, books, and music, there are TV shows such as the *Lifestyles of the Rich and Famous* from the 1980s and 1990s and the current reality TV wasteland glorifying celebrity lifestyles, rich housewives, expensive weddings, and over-the-top coming-of-age parties.

Upon arrival in the Land of Wealth, Assimilators fling off their middle-class trappings in favor of luxurious possessions and extravagant activities. Homes are traded up, as are cars and sometimes spouses. Interiors are redecorated in the latest styles, in ever-changing fashion. Children are enrolled in the best private schools, hopefully from preschool onward, and there is a constant emphasis on appearance, luxury, and success.

———

When the Morgans received their $47 million, Max indulged his passion for all things mechanical—sports cars, motorcycle racing, high-end shotguns, fancy watches. Adrienne lavished money on jewelry, clothing, vacations, and her favorite activity—decorating. They immediately began planning their dream home, hiring expensive architects to design the grand extras they had always wanted. As construction proceeded, they kept adding new features that drove up the cost.

They especially enjoyed the social scene they now were invited into, meeting people they recognized from the news. Max started getting inside tips on investment opportunities from prominent business leaders. Adrienne's financial support of an entourage of friends and family members helped secure her a constant stream of attention.

In their minds, there was no reason to be careful. They figured that happiness would come from leaving behind their life on the edge of debt. They were free, or so they thought. As Adrienne told her best friend from high school, "the money feels, well, infinite!" They didn't realize that even $47 million could be drained by poor choices and habits.

———

WHERE AVOIDERS CLING TO THE PAST, ASSIMILATORS ABANDON it. Assimilators discard their former values, identity, and whatever healthy constraints might have existed in favor of embracing a lavish lifestyle. Assimilators seem to forget the lessons and values learned under more difficult conditions. One example is the portrayal of Jackie Siegel, the wife in the documentary *The Queen of Versailles*[59] who buys more and more possessions for the largest mansion in America despite the increasingly tenuous state of the family's finances.

For Assimilators, there is only the present, and the future. As a result, they are susceptible to making very poor financial decisions and rapidly deporting themselves—and their families—back to the middle-class life they left behind.

Motivations for Choosing Assimilation

For many newcomers to economic paradise, the motivation to jump in with both feet is completely understandable. There is tremendous relief at having escaped the stresses inherent in a financially constrained life. It's not unusual for most newly wealthy Immigrants to do an initial burst of spending on long-overdue or long-desired possessions. Once this phase passes, the spending settles back down closer to the baseline rate of purchases that existed before. Most individuals return to what feels most comfortable from their prior habits and money personality. If an Immigrant spends freely for a limited period of time and then moves on to a more measured approach, Assimilation can be a fling that eventually leads to a balanced set of coping strategies.

What distinguishes Immigrants who choose Assimilation as a long-term strategy is that indulgence continues to rule the day. Only too happy to have arrived, these newcomers in paradise want nothing more to do with middle-class life or identity. They don't just want to live more comfortably among the wealthy; they want to *belong*.

———

Max Morgan felt torn between wanting to show off his newfound wealth to his folks back home and not wanting to revisit his painful roots. Going back to the neighborhood where he grew up made him feel embarrassed of who he really was, at least in his mind. He also worried he would be seen by someone from his present life, the only life he wanted to be associated with.

When he did go back, he found he and Adrienne were not very welcome. His father made cutting remarks about their having become "fancy big shots," and seemed unimpressed with the high-end clothes, cars, homes, and trips. When Max offered his father money, he accepted it grudgingly then put it in savings. Max's parents also complained that the Morgans' sons, Alex and Adam, behaved in an entitled and undisciplined manner. Only the eldest daughter, Alicia, seemed unaffected by all the money.

All Max felt about his real background was ashamed, criticized, and misunderstood. He was much more at ease among other executives who treated him like one of them. His trips home grew more infrequent.

———

THEY WANT MONEY TO MAKE THEM HAPPY

Some strangers in paradise are drawn to Assimilation based on the belief that the possessions and experiences wealth can buy will provide an unending stream of pleasure. Undaunted by warnings that money doesn't buy happiness, they subscribe to the wry comment of Spike Milligan, the British entertainer, who once said, "All I ask is the chance to prove that money can't make me happy." Assimilators are convinced a never-ending supply of material goods will bring meaning to their lives, so they try their utmost to make that happen.

A similar motivation is to leave behind circumstances and associations that remain painful or embarrassing. Some Immigrants to the

Land of Wealth have very difficult pasts, particularly associated with money. They are happy to embrace a new identity when the old one feels shameful.

Others make the unfortunate choice of Assimilation because they imbue money and wealth with powerful meaning. In doing so, any and all reflections of having great wealth take on exaggerated significance. If wealth symbolizes success, talent, intelligence, or even superiority, then ostentatious displays play a psychological role in supporting their self-esteem. Their egos become bound up in being a member of what they always admired as the culture of wealth.

———

Adrienne Morgan had been raised in what she thought was an upper-middle-class family who ran an upscale women's clothing store. Both her parents worked long hours, so, in their guilt over not being around as much as other parents, they often brought her gifts and indulged her with whatever she wanted. She also didn't have limits imposed on her like many of her friends. From an early age, she learned to associate money and lack of discipline with being special.

In reality, Adrienne's parents chronically spent well beyond their means. They finally had to declare bankruptcy when she was in college. She was never able to finish her education and had to take secretarial and modeling jobs in order to support herself. In marrying Max, she believed she found someone who would again coddle her, let her do what she wanted, and give her everything she was supposed to have. His success in selling the company was the proof she always wanted that she was special.

———

THEY NEED VISIBLE PROOF OF THEIR WORTH

Assimilation provides some economic Immigrants constant reassurance that their success is deserved. Some Pioneers and many Transplants don't believe they've legitimately arrived in the Land of Wealth. They feel like imposters and expect to be sent back at any moment to where they really belong. Assimilation is how they shore up their own recognition and acceptance of their economic success. Or, they worry that other people will question their right to belong in the wealth culture. Their exaggerated adoption of their new social world is a strategy to secure their place, as if they must constantly demonstrate to themselves, and others, that they deserve to be counted among the wealthy.

A somewhat related but more understandable motivation applies to less-advantaged groups making their way to wealth. Some wealthy women, people of color, and members of other nontraditional groups choose Assimilation as a way to feel vindicated. Because they have often been historically barred from wealth, achieving great financial success may feel like a rebuttal to the messages they received about inferiority and exclusion. Prominently displaying their wealth conveys a message to the world that they have overcome prejudices and are paving the way for others to follow. In a society that saturates its members with the idea that wealth symbolizes triumph, this visible use of wealth can signal an individual or group sense of pride in the process.

THEY WANT TO GAIN NEW COMMUNITY

Just as Avoiders refuse to break old ties in order to adapt, some Assimilators are more than happy to form new ties in a community willing to welcome them. Wealth is a ready-made ticket into some social circles founded largely on the shared history of making it to paradise. Where previously an individual was just one among many in middle-class life, he or she is now one among a special few in the culture of wealth. The shared journey of immigration to the Land of Wealth makes for useful commonalities, even if there are few other experiences or traits in common.

THEY LACK MONEY SKILLS FOR BETTER COPING

Some wealth Immigrants are susceptible to Assimilation due to deficits in financial skills. They may have achieved remarkable business success in their work life, perhaps through a successful company that goes public or gets bought out. But in their personal lives, they may never have grasped, for example, that crucial distinction between *money-as-asset* versus *money-as-income*. Coming out of the middle class, they are ecstatic at the new freedom of a large income. But they fail to understand their role in now having to manage the assets behind that income.

When money starts pouring in, these economic newcomers are

unprepared to handle such wealth capably. With luck they may look to others to manage it for them, but even in delegating these responsibilities to advisors, they often fail to appreciate the role they must take in working with, not against, professional advice.

———

Max and Adrienne were the worst kind of clients to the advisors they chose. They accumulated a hodgepodge of CPAs, insurance agents, private bankers, investment advisors, attorneys, financial planners, and anyone else who made a good pitch for their services. Max thought that "diversification" meant not putting too much money in the hands of any one advisor. The result was that many of the Morgans' investments overlapped, were inefficient, or even worked against each other. No one advisor knew the whole picture, so there was no quarterback who could see and integrate the process. As a result, excessive fees ate away a good portion of whatever investment performance was achieved.

The hidden motivation was that Max and Adrienne secretly took advantage of the fact no advisor really knew what was going on with their spending. By keeping advisors splintered, they were able to do what they wanted without anyone noticing or bringing up the issue.

———

The Perils of Assimilation

What's wrong with enjoying wealth so dramatically, especially considering how fleeting success can be? Why not throw open the door to wealth rather than keep the latch bolted and padlocked?

The reasons are equivalent to the problems associated with the one-sided strategy of Avoidance. Both approaches react to stereotypes—formulated and perpetuated by those who are not really in a position to know—about "The Rich." They become those inhabitants of *Richistan*, Robert Frank's scathing portrayal of the modern American Land of Wealth.[60] By abandoning the beneficial aspects of a middle-class heritage, Assimilation damages the present functioning of G1 Immigrants and plants the seeds of destruction for G2 and G3 Natives.

THEY SUFFER AN EROSION OF VALUES

Chasing wealth's pleasures and possessions without a grounding in healthy values leads to the very qualities for which too much money is notorious: self-centeredness, entitlement, a lack of concern for the social benefits wealth can accomplish, and a lack of perspective about the true value of material things.

To friends or family still living a middle-class life, Assimilators appear to become either pompous or conveniently forgetful of their humble beginnings. In doing so, Assimilators fulfill the dual stereotypes held by society that a) "The Rich" are shallow people lacking values or perspective, and b) having money destroys people.

THEY GO OVERBOARD WITH CHARITY

An interesting phenomenon I've observed with many overspending Assimilators is a seemingly paradoxical tendency to be very philanthropic. They are highly generous to family, friends, religious organizations, educational institutions, and other noble causes, even when rapidly burning through their assets. Why would someone devoted to excessive spending waste money on charity?

The answers lie again in the mindset of those wanting to act "richer than 'The Rich.'" Philanthropic work is highly associated with being wealthy, the benefits of which include attending gala events, making large donations, accepting invitations to serve on foundations, and enjoying recognition as a philanthropist. It matters little whether the impulse to give charitably is heartfelt or just an obligation adopted by newcomers wanting to fit in. A side benefit is that it feeds the egos of Assimilators wanting recognition they "have arrived." Unfortunately it also makes them targets for both legitimate and unscrupulous charitable organizations.

A little-known characteristic of many who overspend in general is a tendency to be overly charitable, whether in middle-class life or wealth. Overspenders who should be more prudent with their money should also be careful about extravagant charitable contributions. But they resist making wise decisions in this, just as in other areas of their spending. There is also a big plus to big philanthropy. Overspenders cleverly use their generous charitable giving as proof they obviously are not self-centered overspenders. Grand philanthropy can be remarkably effective in silencing critics who start to question how you spend your money.

THEY ARE AT RISK FOR ADDICTIONS

Assimilation is closely associated with emotionally driven spending patterns that have much in common with addictions.[61] There are many similarities between the pleasure-seeking cycles of substance abuse and the compulsive cycles seen in gambling and overspending. With more money comes greater capacity to indulge in these patterns. At higher levels of wealth, strangers in paradise may be insulated, at least for a while, from the consequences of their overspending. But the patterns themselves are inherently the same, and eventually the consequences do catch up to the wealthy overspender.

Addictive money patterns also tend to breed other addictions, whether chemical dependencies (alcohol and drug abuse), gambling, certain types of eating disorders, or sexual addictions. Access to plentiful resources, combined with contact with other individuals with addictive disorders, increases the risk of dangerous behavioral patterns that can be hard to break. One common stereotype of the wealthy has some basis in fact: Portrayals of the wildly indulgent wealthy almost always include heavy drinking, drug use, and promiscuity, at the very least.

———

The Morgans were growing increasingly worried about their middle son Alexander, now approaching his mid-twenties. They had always given him a generous allowance each month, which he was supposed to use as support while completing the end of his drawn-out college education. They also paid his apartment rent, all utilities and insurances, and his car repair bills for his occasional accidents. Their rationale was that they didn't want him to have the extra stress of having to work while trying to complete his education. And, after all, they had the money.

The problem was that, always one to party since high school, Alex's drug use had accelerated since the family came into its millions. He had been in and out of rehab three times already, and he seemed to have no sense about money. He was constantly pressuring Max and Adrienne for more. The Morgans wanted to believe him when he said he was managing his recovery, though they had doubts. But whenever they would raise the idea of cutting back support, Alex would either accuse them of being cheap or would act agitated, tearful, and anxious. Adrienne was terrified the stress would push him over the edge, so she always backed off. This cycle continued for many years with little change.

———

How Assimilation Impacts the Children

The strategy of Assimilation further damages the family by leaving the next generation unanchored from important values and skills commonly forged by economic hardship. Even though it may appear that these children live an ideal life, filled with abundance and security, the psychological ramifications of the Assimilation approach can be significant.

THEY DEVELOP DISTORTED SELF-ESTEEM

The offspring of Assimilators suffer from a lack of grounded values and a distorted sense of self-esteem. Their lot is what society associates with the shallow, purposeless wealthy. The common denominator is that wealth is a dominating influence in the home and therefore in their life and identity. It is hard to develop properly in the shade of such an overpowering presence. Without good parenting to provide guidance, personality adjustment can take several unfortunate directions.

One response is to become highly self-centered and spoiled. The personalities of these Natives of wealth have strong components of narcissism, a syndrome that includes an insecure yet inflated self-esteem, a lack of empathy for other people's feelings or needs, a sense of entitlement, and a tendency toward grandiose plans which may or may not ever come to fruition. These G2s believe they should have whatever they desire and become agitated when denied it. This pattern is particularly damaging to relationships, since their capacity to truly understand and attend to other people's needs is quite limited.

Another direction is to become susceptible to chronic depression, anxiety, and guilt. These offspring of Assimilators struggle with the same problems with self-esteem, but instead of responding to their

inner hollowness with outward grandiosity, they sink into discourage-
ment, insecurity, and fragility.

Appendix II touches upon the many elements of parenting needed
to nurture healthy children in an environment of wealth. Suffice it to
say that parents taking an Assimilation approach let wealth get in the
way of developing their children's initiative, frustration tolerance, ability to delay gratification, and empathy for others.

THEY EXPERIENCE CONFLICTING MESSAGES

Assimilator parents may make token attempts at instilling restraint and
preventing entitlement, but these efforts are half-hearted and inconsis-
tent. Children are told to manage their allowance, but they aren't given
limits for online purchases of music or clothing, which can be substantial. They are admonished to remember how lucky they are, and then
they are deluged at holidays and birthdays with an escalating cycle of
expensive presents, reinforcing a sense of being special. When children
whine at not getting what they want, the parents give in but then blame
the child for acting spoiled.

The problem is that it's hard to deny your children luxuries if you
see no reason to impose restraint on yourself. Some high-living parents believe they can teach responsibility and humility by simply telling
their kids to be responsible or humble—the "do what I say, not what I
do" philosophy. Yet as fellow wealth counselor Thayer Willis has aptly
written, "the most important values in life are caught, not taught."[62]
Modeling good financial decision-making, balance, self-restraint, or
self-responsibility must go along with the words.

———

The Morgans' young son Adam sat watching TV with his best friend in
the family room of the Morgans' McMansion, surrounded by enough
toys to stock a toy store. They channel-surfed to a cable TV rerun of a
reality TV show in which a well-dressed young mother took her children
shoe shopping for school. The kids in the show wandered unsupervised
throughout the store while the mother was engrossed in trying on shoes
for herself. She eventually narrowed her options to two pairs of expensive shoes. Unable to decide which pair to buy, she said gaily, "Well, you
know what they say, 'when in doubt, buy both!'"

Adam and his friend smiled knowingly at each other. They'd seen similar behavior and heard their own mothers say the exact same thing many times. As an inside joke, they began mimicking the phrase "when in doubt, buy both!" in stores themselves. However, the message about financial decision-making stuck.

———

THEY DON'T LEARN FISCAL RESPONSIBILITY

The deadliest words in the world of wealth are: "I don't want my kids to suffer the way I did." Parents happy to be released from economic hardship forget that they were also formed by that hardship, building their perspectives and their knowledge of how the world works. Since Assimilators seek to leave behind their roots as completely as possible, they also abandon reasonable and necessary conditions that teach money skills.

On a practical level, these G2s, and eventually G3s, lag in developing the component skills needed for a financially responsible life. Because their Immigrant parents or grandparents are focused on the trappings of wealth rather than managing and sustaining wealth, these Natives have little exposure to learning healthy money skills or financial decision-making.

I work with many multigenerational ultra-high-net-worth (UHNW) families fighting over widespread overspending and poor communication. In one such family, the wealth-creating G1s—overspenders dating back to the dot-com era—abruptly changed their minds about supporting any and all educational expenses for the family. They felt their college-age grandchildren, who thought nothing of dropping out after tuition had already been paid (and forfeited), were abusing their generosity. These G3s then expected to return to school later with full support again, no questions asked. The grandparents didn't realize that they, like many fortunate families, had trained everyone to expect support in whatever they wanted, especially those wonderfully tax-advantaged medical and educational expenses.

The problem was that few people in G2 or G3 knew what to do if somebody in the family didn't pay educational expenses. One daughter, Marisa, believed that if her parents didn't pay for her son's college bill, her only choice was to do so from her own money. She was focused on how unfair that was and how to get her parents to back their original promises. "Marisa, what do middle-class people do if they want to go back to school and they don't have family money to support them?" I asked. Marisa frowned, looked away for a long moment, and then looked back. She said quietly, "I don't know. What do they do?"

I walked Marisa through a basic lesson in student loans, grants, and work-study opportunities. I reminded her that her son could first spend some time building up a college account by working. We discussed how she could match those funds or let him discover just how valuable tuition money feels when it is saved toward a goal. We also talked over the utility of her son having some investment (emotionally and financially) in his own education. It was an eye-opening conversation for a person of wealth, someone who literally did not know what many people learn out of necessity in American middle-class culture.

THEY LEARN TO EQUATE MONEY WITH PROBLEM-SOLVING

Parents diving into wealth typically use money to handle whatever stresses come up in their own lives. They also wind up using money as the panacea for any relationship stress, life obstacle, parental absence, child-rearing problem, or parental inadequacy. Where parents using an Avoidance strategy have difficulty spending money for even reasonable needs, parents using an Assimilation strategy enlist money for virtually everything. In doing so, Assimilators train G2s to associate money with love, caring, problem solving, and conflict management. Aside from damaging G2's life skills, it sets the stage for relationship stresses and parenting difficulties when it comes time for G2 to parent G3.

THEIR RELATIONSHIPS REVOLVE AROUND MONEY

When parents chose Assimilation, wealth gets wired into the dynamics of the family. Financial support, inheritance, favoritism, and jockeying for position all revolve around the central role of wealth in the family. Parents learn to exercise control by offering or withholding money, or even by implying they will do one or the other.

As a result, children quickly learn to be attuned to secrets, hints, or implications about family relationships played out through money. No matter who is favored or pushed away, all siblings become sensitive to real or perceived injustices, keeping a running tally of where everyone ranks in the family hierarchy. This tendency toward emotional accounting then invades their adult relationships outside the family.

Without the compass provided by the best aspects of middle-class values and skills, the children of Assimilators are not taught how to navigate the natural storms of any adult life, or the unique stresses of affluence. When they go astray, they are viewed as proof that character does get poisoned when the family becomes rich.

How Assimilation Impacts Estate Planning

While those who opt for Avoidance may have more than enough assets to bequeath to succeeding generations, those who opt for Assimilation are at risk for having not much left. They may—consciously or unconsciously—do their best to spend all of the money before they die. Other options are not very good, either.

THEY PROCRASTINATE UNTIL THE END

Like Avoiders who let the chips fall where they may, some Assimilators just cannot face estate planning and the long-term thinking required. Despite the best efforts of advisors, these G1 wealth-holders never get around to putting pen to paper for long-term planning.

Some don't want to think about what happens to their money once they are gone. They have been so focused on becoming wealthy that they are unprepared to look toward the horizon where the wealth out-lives them. Some are too busy focusing on the present—and their own needs—to plan for the future. Some continue their avoidance of tough decisions, as they did in childrearing. For all these reasons, the money gets put at risk due to failure to plan well. As a result, taxes, probate costs, and state laws get to dictate what happens

———

Eight years after the sale of SteriMetrix, the Morgans' money was going from "infinite" to under $25 million. Overspending, bad investment decisions in unsettled markets, and a few persuasive but unscrupulous

brokers had taken their toll. Max and Adrienne switched to yet another
wealth management team to stabilize things. This time they were willing to consolidate their affairs, primarily because they were feeling more
than a little scared.

   One action the new team strongly recommended was to get better
estate planning in place. The Morgans' last estate plan had been written
before SteriMetrix had been sold. Their youngest child was approaching
eighteen, tax laws had changed, and concerns about their sons' spending were growing. Only their eldest daughter Alicia seemed responsible,
but relations with her were strained. Max and Adrienne faced hard decisions as their new trusts-and-estates attorney walked them through their
options. Planning dragged on for years because they felt paralyzed about
what to do.

THEY DEPLETE THEIR ASSETS

A common outcome is that estate planning is in place, but the money
is depleted by the time inheritance occurs. The pressure to support the
family's excessive spending consumes the parents' assets, piles on debt,
and sometimes even spills over to unwise decisions in a family business,
decisions which doom the business itself.

   Well in advance of inheritance, G1s become the enablers of some or
all in G2 (and G3) who expect their parents to fulfill all of their money
needs, no matter how irresponsible or unending. The twin demons of
entitlement and materialism then devour the family's money. Disap-
pointment and resentment become the real legacy passed on to G2
and G3 by Assimilators as the family gets deported from the Land
of Wealth. Ironically, the next generation has to learn to survive in
a culture they were not raised in, completing the cycle and fulfilling
shirtsleeves-to-shirtsleeves.

THEY HAND OVER THE MONEY

Another estate-planning decision by Assimilators is that G2 and/or G3
receive a direct inheritance, not in trust. These G1s perpetuate the pattern of funneling money to their children with little or no preparation

to manage the windfall. G2 is left on its own to repeat, modify, or reject what they learned from their parents' shortsighted adjustment to wealth.

This has several consequences for the next generation. For those children and grandchildren who haven't been taught the necessary financial skills, inheritance is likely to prove disastrous. Unless they have learned a better way to handle money from advisors, friends, responsible family members, therapists, or other sources of support, they are likely to repeat the mistakes of their parents' generation. They too fulfill shirtsleeves-to-shirtsleeves in record time.

Those who wind up learning some financial self-management skills —even if they had to seek it as an adult—can actually do reasonably well. I've seen and helped many G2s find their way toward better financial skills, relationship patterns, and self-esteem, despite the unfortunate examples of how their parents handled wealth. Responsible G2s who grow up with Assimilators must remake their own adjustment to wealth in healthier ways—or risk deportation.

THEY CREATE ANIMOSITY AMONG SIBLINGS

An extra stress, however, is that G2s who take a prudent approach to personal finances can find themselves emotionally or financially chained to siblings who are replicating their parents' bad habits. It's not hard to imagine what happens when overspending siblings start to run out of money: They turn to family members who still have theirs. The irresponsible ones pressure their brothers and sisters to take over the enabling established by their parents. Responsible ones are then faced with extremely difficult choices about whether to help their own flesh and blood. The legacy of G1s' Assimilation approach can be years of frustration, guilt, jealousy, pleading, entitlement, and anger amongst siblings.

THEY GIVE IT AWAY, FOR GOOD OR ILL

Making philanthropy "the other child" in estate planning is, as always, an option for Immigrants choosing Assimilation. Some reasons are better than others. Sometimes G1s finally want to stop enabling. Sometimes they turn against their children in anger over their apparent overspending. Sometimes G1 decides it would be noble to leave a substantial

portion of whatever remains to charitable causes. Philanthropic giving may therefore be an act of punishment to the family or a last-gasp
attempt at redeeming the family name.

This infuriates G2s who expect to receive what they feel is rightfully
theirs. Many adult children of Assimilators spend their lives so preoc-
cupied with wealth that they have strong feelings about what should be
done with the money when their turn comes. Philanthropy is not often
part of that plan. Ironically, those responsible children who have been
repulsed by the family's materialism may be relieved to see the money
go to society where it will finally do some good.

THEY PASS ON THE MONEY IN TRUST

Many Assimilators choose to bequeath in trust whatever is left of their
estate. Using trusts makes sense on many levels. Trusts are, after all,
what are typically done for estate planning with the wealthy, so this
fits in with the prevailing culture. It is a badge of honor to be wealthy
enough to set up trusts for the children, plus everyone else at the country club is doing it. Where the rub comes is in the design and imple-
mentation of the trust.

Parents with irresponsible children are usually willing to create
trusts at least to protect money from creditors and grasping spouses,
or to maximize tax benefits. The question is whether the parents have
insight that their children's behavior was largely their fault and now
requires limit setting.

One camp—enabling to the end—permits generous distributions by
the trustee to "preserve the beneficiary's lifestyle." This is a nightmare
for any responsible trustee to implement. But, as long as the trust-cre-
ator's intent is clear and trustee liability for allowing depletion of assets
is limited, it certainly reduces fights with beneficiaries.

The difficulty comes when Assimilators decide to clamp down on
irresponsible behavior. Some realize as time goes on that they neither
modeled nor taught good financial behaviors and didn't set necessary
limits on irresponsible behaviors. Believing any hope for change will
have to come from delegating limit-setting to someone else, they punt
at the end, choosing trustees more capable of saying "no" than they
were themselves. Others remain in denial about their lack of effective

parenting. Instead, they blame their children, or society, or money itself for ruining their kids. This is a perfect example of strangers who arrive in paradise without a clue about what to do correctly and then blame others—anyone but themselves—for the outcome. In either case, trusts are then written with limits around self-destructive financial behavior to a greater or lesser extent.

Children of overspenders make particularly terrible beneficiaries of such trusts. They don't understand why or how trustees may exert reasonable control over their persistent requests for distributions of income or principal. They naturally accuse trustees of being overly controlling. And so, of course, they are quick to litigate when they don't get what they feel entitled to have. The dysfunctional family dynamics then get extended to contentious trustee-beneficiary relationships that frustrate everyone involved.

The Challenges of Assimilation

Those strangers in paradise devoted to an Assimilation strategy fully expect they will find comfort and identity within a culture they admired from afar. Just as those choosing Avoidance believe only the worst about wealth, those choosing Assimilation believe only the best, or that they can somehow sidestep wealth's risks.

Ultimately, money cannot provide all that Assimilators hope it might. Those beneficial attitudes, skills, and values forged in working-class or middle-class life have great worth. Immigrants to paradise are well advised to retain the values of work ethic, self-responsibility, self-discipline, perseverance in the face of stress, and willingness to take reasonable risks. They also need to learn that the culture of wealth goes well beyond materialism and indulgence. If they want successive generations to handle the family's resources well and continue a productive legacy, they need to teach a full set of healthy values to their children and grandchildren.

There is a better approach to handling the stresses and tasks of acculturating to wealth. As with ethnic immigrants, the strategy is clear: Retain the core values of the heritage culture while learning the healthy rules of the new homeland. In attempting integration of the two cultures in one's identity and behavior, Immigrants to wealth have the opportunity to navigate the transition effectively. They also keep the family on a path more likely to lead to success for the future.

CHAPTER 7

Integration: The Best of Both Worlds

There are few portrayals in literature, TV, or film of first-generation wealth-holders handling their newfound fortune in a moderate, well-balanced way. Their lives don't manifest intriguing drama. [63]

Thankfully, real life offers us positive examples. There are many successful Pioneers around the world who seem to strike a balance between
their heritage identity and the new world of wealth they inhabit: Oprah
Winfrey, Warren Buffett, Charles Schwab, and J.K. Rowling are a few
of the more well-known names. There are thousands of others, including many I have met while providing consultation services to families
of wealth.

I would estimate, in fact, that the majority of clients I've counseled
over the years have been hoping to find productive ways to integrate
where they came from and where they now are. Most have been trying
to navigate a middle ground between what they learned growing up,
what they still believe, and what they must do to understand their corner of economic paradise.

———

As the tidal wave of money and attention poured into their lives, Phil and
Barb Spinelli tried to manage their many reactions: euphoria, fear, mistrust, disorientation, poor concentration, giddiness. They didn't know
how to think about themselves or what was happening. It seemed everyone around them was happy for them, with lots of unsolicited advice.
Few people really understood the whirlwind of emotions Phil and Barb
were experiencing, which made them strongly devoted to taking time to
process things together. They shared ideas and reactions with each other,
tried to keep life as steady as possible for themselves and their daughters,
and committed themselves to finding the best advice they could about
handling sudden wealth.

Through their research, the Spinellis learned their experience was typical, and likely to last longer than they assumed. They created a "decision-
free zone" for themselves by parking their newfound fortune in cash
for six months. This gave them time to orient to their new environment
before, in a sense, putting down roots. They also spent time talking to
their daughters Gina and Stephanie about how the whirlwind affected
the girls' lives. As a result, the family drew closer as events unfolded.

How Integration Manifests in the Land of Wealth

The natural course of adjustment for many ethnic immigrants is the
third option for acculturation, what cross-cultural psychology refers
to as Integration or biculturalism (Figure 7-1). Ethnic newcomers to a
place or a culture weave together strands from the old life and new life
into a fresh identity and a new set of behaviors and attitudes. When
successful, Integration helps them feel whole, empowered, and confident they will make the best decisions for themselves and their families.

This type of adjustment is common for cross-cultural families. An

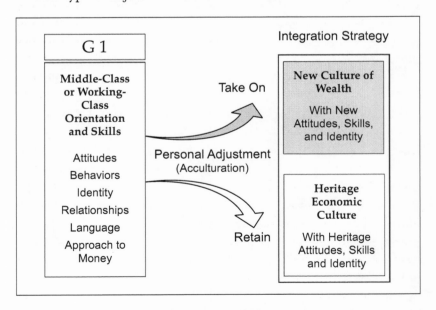

Figure 7-1: The acculturation strategy of Integration.

example might be a lower-middle-class Latino couple from Mexico who come to Boston and adopt American habits and language, yet continue to celebrate (literally and emotionally) the holidays and achievements of their forebears. They raise well-grounded, successful children fluent in Spanish, English, and middle-class American life. Another example would be an Asian family from Shanghai that migrates to San Francisco so their children can be born American while still being raised with the wisdom of their Chinese heritage. Though the family initially lives in the Chinatown district, over time, as they gain financial security and more experience with a blended Chinese-American culture, they move to the suburbs where they become even more adapted to American life.

Why does society understand this approach with ethnic immigrants, yet fail to grasp that it is equally possible for the wealthy? For wealth's Pioneers or Transplants, an Integration strategy naturally tries to combine the reality of being a person of wealth alongside a core identity of having come from middle- or working-class roots. The old and the new are not as incompatible as those choosing Avoidance or Assimilation may think, and the result can be much more satisfying.

I worked with Sam and Angie, for example, who met in a middle-class New Jersey high school. They now are co-owners of a prospering real estate business worth more than $110 million. They work hard to feel as comfortable with their friends from the old neighborhood as they do with their new peers in the world of investment real estate. They are raising their young children to move comfortably between their private-school world and the family's Italian-American roots. Their goals are to prepare their children to manage their allowances responsibly now and whatever wealth will come into their lives later.

Then there is Jorge, a man very much feeling like a stranger in paradise as he tries to integrate his childhood identity and his new success. Jorge went from laboring in a landscape-supply business to owning a prominent farmland management enterprise in the Southwest. He and his male partner are supporting local initiatives for teaching urban community-college students organic farming methods. Jorge's favorite activity is sharing his own background with the students and inspiring them to work hard and aim high, as he did.

And there is Helena, who thought she found her life's work as the only craftswoman in her father's furniture-making business. She discovered her real calling when she had to take over and expand the business significantly after her father died prematurely. She became one of the wealthiest businesswomen in the state. Her quiet, taciturn nature didn't lend itself to talking much about her values, but every one of her children learned the continuing family ethic of hard work, perseverance, humility, and sharing from observing their mother's integration into her new role and status.

Motivations for Choosing Integration

Integration is easy to understand though sometimes hard to accomplish. It requires willingness on the part of the Immigrant to experiment, to learn, and to be open to change. It grows from the desire to maintain some degree of cultural continuity while gradually participating in the social and cultural networks to which he or she has migrated.[64] This requires a long process of negotiating with others and with oneself what must be newly learned and what can—and often should—be carried forth productively from one's past.

For many Immigrants, the process is a workable blending of the old and the new over time. For a few, Integration leads to a qualitatively higher level, one that rises above standard thinking about either culture to a fuller, deeper perspective on what wealth and life can be.

THEY WANT A HEALTHY AND PRODUCTIVE ADJUSTMENT

The motivations for Integration focus on adjusting in flexible, adaptive ways to wealth, minus the limiting—and often hidden—motivations that drive the more one-sided strategies of Avoidance and Assimilation. Individuals wanting to integrate their old and new cultures are primarily motivated by:

- The desire to retain cherished relationships and common bonds.
- The desire to make new, healthy relationships based on shared interests and common experiences.
- The willingness to accept a new identity in the world, hiding from neither who they are nor who they were.

- The desire not to let temptation and pleasure dissolve the values learned in adversity.

Juggling the familiar and the novel, Integrators craft a bicultural identity and set of skills supporting the long-term goal of change: Adaptation. They are willing to answer those two questions of acculturation (who am I? what group do I belong to?) with the complexity natural to their situation. They don't have to manufacture a simple answer for a complicated question.

Strangers in paradise who opt for Integration have some of the same motivations mentioned in prior chapters, but they are willing to consider solutions in a more finely grained manner:

- They allow themselves legitimate pride in their achievement and success, *and* they remember that success typically springs from the contributions of many people and factors.

- They enjoy the benefits of their wealth, *and* their self-esteem is not so dependent on their possessions. They don't require wealth to provide proof of their worth to the world or themselves. They know that money can provide pleasure and ease, yet they don't demand that it delivers happiness.

- In seeking answers to the "Who am I? question, Integrators may focus more what brought them to paradise than their badge of citizenship. This is particularly true for Pioneers, who work hard over years, providing for their families and building their businesses, only to discover that, somewhere along the way, they crossed over into the Land of Wealth. Their identity is much more tied up in being successful than in being wealthy.

This fundamental tolerance for complexity may be the hallmark of those choosing Integration. It is also what contributes to their adaptability, a key factor that will be discussed at length in the subsequent chapters on Adaptation.

THEY WANT TO FIND COMMUNITY

Integrators considering the second question of acculturation—"To which group do I belong?"—tend to be more willing to accept answers in the plural: To which *groups* do I belong? They are able to hold onto some old relationships while finding new ones in a gradual process over time. I've observed that individuals taking an Integration approach naturally gravitate to others taking the same approach, if they can find each other among the many social networks of wealth. The group they feel most comfortable belonging to seems to be the group of newly wealthy adapting in a similar manner.

———

The Spinellis allowed themselves a period of some indulgence, socially and financially. They attended more social engagements, upgraded their cars to luxury models, and made some long-overdue home improvements, using higher-quality materials and contractors than they would've used before. These all felt strange for a while, until Phil and Barb became used to them.

They also found themselves getting bored or disillusioned with many of the new people they met. When they did meet particularly interesting couples who seemed down-to-earth and intelligent, the Spinellis would follow up with personal invitations to dinner or an evening out together. Throughout it all, they still spent time with their old friends and family, just as they had before.

———

FINDING COMMUNITY MAY BE EASIER FOR SOME ETHNIC AND economic immigrants than others. Cross-cultural psychology teaches that ease of acculturation partly depends on the goodness-of-fit between the immigrant and his or her new environment. Integration is most possible and smooth when the match is close, as in language, customs, attitudes, and even appearance. Integration is less easy when the alignment between old and new is difficult to bridge.

Making the broad leap from a working-class background to affluence is especially stressful. Alfred Lubrano, the author of *Limbo: Blue Collar Roots, White Collar Dreams,*[65] provides an articulate description of the uniquely difficult adjustment of bridging that gap. Lubrano writes of his years trying to integrate a Brooklyn working-class background with an upscale college education and a subsequent white-collar career.

He labels himself and others like him, "Straddlers." The term captures nicely his lifelong sense of having one foot firmly planted in his blue-collar background and one foot in the affluent world to which he migrated.

Lubrano's phrase for integrating the old and the new is "duality," which he associates with a never-ending struggle with identity.[66] Consistent with the themes in this book, he advises that "[i]deally, a Straddler becomes bicultural. Understand what made you who you are, then learn to navigate the new setting."[67] It takes a capacity for holding seemingly incompatible beliefs simultaneously until a new understanding emerges from the turmoil. Those who are able to tolerate the struggle eventually find their way to a growing awareness of themselves and their new life. They also may find community with others who've made the same journey.

THEY WANT TO BUILD COMMUNITY

Finding others of similar background is also easier for some strangers in paradise. Some traditionally marginalized groups of wealth who want to retain their identity yet openly belong to wealth have to work harder at creating the best of both worlds. Predominantly white male, heterosexual networks of wealth have typically not been very welcoming to newcomers who don't fit aspects of their profile. Successful women, people of color, lesbian/gay/bisexual/transgendered (LGBT), and other ethnically or racially diverse individuals must be strongly motivated to find their place at the table using an Integration strategy. They have to work at integrating different economic cultures in their identity internally, while simultaneously dealing with discrimination externally.

The coming decades should witness a dramatic shift in the ability of some disadvantaged groups to integrate more successfully in the culture of wealth. This is due both to their increasing numbers and to finally having greater support from advisors. Women are accelerating in the three fundamental drivers of wealth creation: education, entrepreneurship, and earnings.[68] All three factors are increasing the number of women who become wealthy in their own right, beyond their traditional avenues of inheriting assets from husbands or parents. Wealth management firms are paying attention to this trend. They are devoting greater resources and creating specialized units for the needs of these independent, entrepreneurial women.

The same is happening for the LGBT population. Prominent wealth firms such as Northern Trust, Morgan Stanley, and UBS have created teams oriented to nontraditional investors. The College for Financial Planning (CFP) has begun offering a new designation of Accredited Domestic Partnership Advisor. Smaller firms are joining the trend as they see the market opportunities.

Cross-cultural psychology tells us that even moderately resilient multicultural societies find ways of making room for the groups they take in. They adapt in reciprocal fashion to the immigrants arriving at their shores. As wealth gradually becomes more global and diverse, Integration may be available as a coping strategy to more strangers making it to paradise.

THEY WANT TO INSURE THEIR CHILDREN'S WELFARE

One of the strongest motivations to choose Integration concerns the next generation. Thoughtful, responsible parents want to provide helpful guidance to their children and grandchildren about the family's core values and beliefs, while incorporating the reality that the family does live with affluence. G2s and G3s exposed to an affluent lifestyle while growing up are naturally shaped by that environment. Depending on the family's current level of wealth, the next generation may need to be prepared for wealth, or it may simply need to be well-prepared to be middle-class. Either way, the guidance they receive from parents experienced in both cultures is invaluable in that preparation.

Newly wealthy parents must respond flexibly as they see the next generation living a life significantly more affluent than they themselves experienced. Compared to Avoiders or Assimilators, Integrators approach parenting with a willingness to adapt to fulfill what the family needs, now and for the future.

———

Phil and Barb faced a big decision when their daughter Stephanie was ready for high school. Most of the top-notch private schools were boarding schools, far away. This was very foreign to their own experiences growing up with family dinners and having parents at school events and athletic games. They fretted about letting her go. The schools were truly terrific and they both valued education very highly. But how much did she still need to be with her family? How should they choose between such important needs?

After much discussion, the Spinellis decided to send Stephanie to the nearest excellent private school that offered day-student status. Though they had to drive her 40 minutes each way to the campus, she was home for evenings and weekends, still nestled in family life. They could still supervise her using their fairly strict standards. During her teenage years she could turn to them for guidance instead of a resident advisor who may not be as mature or as focused on Stephanie's individual situation. Best of all, Phil and Barb could share in her remarkable growth, happening right in front of them on a daily basis.

What Contributes to Integration

Compared to the other methods of acculturation, an Integration strategy generally holds the greatest potential for healthy adaptation.[69] With obvious parallels to the world of wealth, research with ethnic immigrants indicates Integration produces individuals who have higher self-esteem, lower rates of depression and adjustment stress, better skills for prospering in their new surroundings, and better ability to make the psychological transition to their new life. It leads to the best outcome for the individual and, in doing so, sets the stage for the best outcome for the family over the long term.

FACTORS FAVORING INTEGRATION

Various factors contribute to the adjustment of wealth's Immigrants. Some pertain to the process of how the wealth was acquired, while others are more characteristic of the person doing the migrating. Most have parallels to the factors influencing the acculturation of ethnic immigrants.

Some of the key differences that impact how a stranger adapts to paradise include:

- **The pace of migration:** All things being equal, having more time to adjust may be an advantage compared to sudden wealth.

The disorientation and abrupt change in culture experienced by wealth's Transplants can severely affect their ability to cope.

- **The degree of forewarning and preparation:** Packing for a journey is easier for most people when they know the timetable and have an idea what they'll need when they arrive at their destination. Short engagements before marriage or sudden liquidity events leave little time for the psychological preparation many people need when facing dramatically new circumstances. Gradual business success culminating in a planned liquidity event, for example, allows more opportunity to acclimate to wealth than winning the lottery.

- **The level of support from family and friends:** Social support is a prime factor in adjusting to stress generally. Individuals with wide support of a positive nature tend to adapt easier than people who are isolated or have to contend with the negative reactions of others.

- **Whether the wealth was earned or unearned:** Broadly speaking, wealth that is personally earned helps people accept their new-found status, build self-esteem, and enjoy the benefits of wealth. Unearned wealth (lottery winnings, marriage, benefiting from others' success in business) tends to induce mixed reactions, including guilt, defensiveness, or experiencing the "imposter syndrome." Unearned wealth also may evoke persistent joking or criticism from others that muddies one's adjustment.

- **Whether the money occurred for positive or negative reasons:** Windfalls that happen as a result of misfortune are very complicated to deal with, as in the case of a large financial settlement resulting from the death of a child or a traumatic event. Although outsiders may be happy about the money, few people enjoy immigrating to paradise as a consequence of terrible situations.

Integration is also impacted by internal factors specific to each immigrant. Two such factors relevant to wealth include:

- **Psychological resilience:** Adaptability is known to rest on a set of positive attributes, such as positive self-esteem, an optimistic worldview, and a flexible set of coping skills. These allow individuals to bounce back from stress more quickly with more resilience than those who are rigid, pessimistic, and/or insecure.

- **Strong-mindedness:** An interesting exception to the issue of psychological rigidity pertains to some wealth creators. They display a certain strong-mindedness that can be unyielding in many ways. Yet their perseverance and single-mindedness is what propels them as entrepreneurs. However, their reluctance to accept input from succeeding generations can make a significant difference in the family's ability to sustain wealth. These Pioneers may adjust to wealth themselves, but they may not adapt very well to the changes necessary for the family to survive.

Factors Challenging Integration

Acculturation is always challenging in regards to relationships. The strategies of Avoidance and Assimilation are, in a way, easier because they are simpler, more black-and-white. Fewer decisions must be made if you always choose one culture over the other. When each situation is faced in all its complexity, the choices are not as obvious.

OLD RELATIONSHIPS BECOME STRAINED

It's not easy to hold onto relationships with middle-class friends once you become wealthy. When high school friends are still struggling financially—with fragile employment, a tough mortgage, and mounting bills—your new life of three homes, complex investments, board meetings, and expensive vacations is truly a different world. The people on both sides of this relationship divide have to contend with the shifting bonds of attachment. Friends or family who once shared common experiences now encounter significant differences in activities, opportunities, perspectives, and attitudes.

Society has typically thought of these stresses between former friends or family and the newly wealthy as the inevitable fallout that occurs when someone becomes rich. These strains are actually a natural dilemma of any migration, ethnic or economic.

CURRENT RELATIONSHIPS CAN BE TESTED

Another common but unanticipated stress occurs when two or more closely tied immigrants adjust in markedly different ways.[70] Relationships founded on shared perspectives in the Old Country may be severely tested in the new adoptive culture. In marriages or sibling relationships, for example, one person may choose one acculturation strategy while his or her partner chooses a different pace or approach. Spouses or siblings willing to integrate elements of the old and new can find themselves rapidly diverging from the attitudes and identities of the ones they love. When this divergence becomes irresolvable, relationships don't survive the migration.

———

As time went on, the strains in Joan and Ted's marriage ballooned. Even invested conservatively, because it was not being tapped, their wealth continued to grow. Joan found herself wanting to use the money to benefit the family, if not themselves. Ted refused, citing the same old arguments: "There's nothing wrong with who we are and how we live. It's a slippery slope to let go of your values even a little. That money could go away tomorrow, just like it did in the Great Depression."

With great difficulty, Joan persuaded Ted to attend a few sessions with a marriage counselor. Ted was willing to talk only generally about their differences over money and Joan's success, but neither of them felt comfortable disclosing the numbers or the real problems. As a result, the therapist was unable to address the underlying issues. After months of little progress, Joan told Ted she wanted a divorce.

The breakup was highly acrimonious. Ted wound up with a generous settlement, taking half of Joan's net worth. She restarted life on her own with a little more than $13 million. Though still financially secure, she felt confused and afraid. She was going to have to find out what her approach to the money would be, no longer yoked to Ted.

———

How Integration Impacts the Children

Immigrants opting for Integration will make choices that impact their parenting, just as with any acculturation strategy. Because of their willingness to consider multiple alternatives, however, these strangers in paradise may have the greatest number of options available to consider.

An Integration strategy provides no guarantee of wonderful parenting or long-term success with family wealth. A great many pitfalls, wrong guesses, and lack of knowledge generate real obstacles to parenting with wealth. Furthermore, if done in a haphazard way over an extended period, a bicultural approach could be confusing to children needing a stable anchor in their upbringing. But if Integration is conducted thoughtfully, in a gradual movement toward a workable strategy, the offspring will largely benefit.

THEY HAVE MORE FLEXIBLE PARENTING

Parents who take time to evaluate multiple choices when acculturation stresses occur are likely to develop the flexibility and resilience needed for raising children and grandchildren in a culture they themselves did not grow up in. This flexibility often shows up in more thoughtful decision-making, better capacity to let children learn via trial and error, and more capacity to discuss issues rather than simply dictate what's right and wrong.

My experience is that Immigrants to wealth who choose an Integration approach demonstrate a quality known by psychologists to support adaptability: *openness*. Openness is a central part of personality, and like all-important traits, ranges from very low (people who are very conventional, closed to new experiences or ideas) to very high (people who are very unconventional, even flighty). Optimal levels fall somewhere near the high-average range.[71] Openness aids adaptation by allowing the thoughtful pursuit of different options, including adaptation in parenting.

Integrators understand that the family and the world around it are changing. They provide a solid grounding in basic tenets of healthy parenting, in values, and in personality development, while also allowing for new experiences and perspectives. They may see the wisdom, for example, in talking about the benefits of wealth in an age-appropriate manner, while still emphasizing the need for work ethic, initiative, purpose, and social consciousness.

THEY FACE FEWER "ACCULTURATION GAPS"

During our teenage and young adult years, we all attempt to answer core questions of identity and affiliation: *Who am I? Where do I belong?* In immigrant families, these normal questions of adolescent development are also the core questions of acculturation.[72] The next generation in immigrant families is attempting to figure out their own social and cultural identities, drawn partly from where the family came from and partly from where the family now lives.

Some tension between the perspectives of parents and their teenage children is natural in all families: the proverbial *generation gap*. Less well known is that it is also natural for immigrant children to adjust to the family's newly adopted culture at a different rate or in a different style from that of their parents. This is an *acculturation gap*.

When the acculturation gap is superimposed on the generation gap, the stress can severely disrupt a crucial period for the second generation. Particularly broad or deep acculturation gaps are known to result in increased risk of substance abuse, conduct problems, anxiety, and depression for vulnerable adolescents in these families.

Acculturation gaps in the second generation of wealth, and perhaps even in the third, may play a larger role than previously imagined in the identity struggles of affluent youth. We know from research studies that there is a higher proportion of substance abuse, anxiety, and depression in affluent youth compared to middle-class or even low-income teenagers.[73] The standard explanations have been that lax parenting, bailing out kids from consequences, and excessive over-scheduling of activities are to blame. Yet contrary to popular belief, the few solid academic studies in this area do not confirm many of these explanations.[74]

The real issues may touch upon the cultural stresses affluent teenagers experience, particularly in G2. Keep in mind that adults who didn't grow up in the culture of affluence and who have only vague ideas about how to guide their children in new circumstances are parenting these G2s. Sticky questions about social and cultural identity surface in ways many parents in G1 frankly misunderstand or are unprepared to answer. When a nine-year-old asks, "Are we rich?" she isn't demanding to see the family's balance sheet. She is seeking legitimate answers to the family's identity and her own. When a fourteen-year-old with both middle-class and affluent friends asks whom he should invite to his birthday celebration, he isn't looking for party planning help. He needs someone to talk him through the complexity of his identity, relationships, and methods for juggling economic diversity.

The question that must be addressed is whether Immigrant parents, fresh off the boat from middle-class life, will be able to answer these questions. Or, will they shut down the conversation due to their own confusion about these very issues? Parents using an Integration strategy are more likely to be able to search for and provide at least some answers their children need. These parents draw from two pools of knowledge—their heritage roots and their current environment—not one. Plus, they are willing to consider new approaches to answer the questions of acculturation for their children.

THEY LEARN THE TRUE NATURE OF PHILANTHROPY

Compared to the tainted nature of philanthropy in homes using an Avoidance or Assimilation approach, charitable giving can be taught and modeled more effectively by parents taking an Integration approach.

Studies of charitable giving find the three biggest areas for philanthropy are religious institutions, educational institutions, and healthcare organizations.[75] There are personal, spiritual, and social motivations for giving to these recipients. There also are the cross-cultural motivations for philanthropy mentioned in earlier chapters: support of old social networks, entrance to new networks, sense of obligation, desire to benefit society at large, or as a badge of acceptance. All apply as well to those choosing Integration as a strategy of adjustment.

Integrators may be more oriented to choosing to acknowledge the origins of their economic migration itself. They take pleasure in supporting others making their own journey to wealth from similar starting places. We hear of the many philanthropic initiatives by Oprah Winfrey, for example, supporting young disadvantaged minorities, especially girls, so they too can rise out of their environment toward success. Ewing Marion Kauffman, the Kansas City area farm boy whose entrepreneurship led to a global diversified healthcare firm, created the

Kauffman Foundation supporting entrepreneurship for others. Many Immigrants to wealth try to leverage their current circumstances to help the culture they came from and still identify with. It can be a way to bridge the two worlds for themselves and for others they hope to bring along.

Philanthropy can also be the next purposeful journey for wealth's Pioneers. Some choose to be serial entrepreneurs, while others shift their focus to investing to achieve social impact or making philanthropic endeavors more efficient or effective. Having arrived in the Land of Wealth (and therefore no longer as driven to make the journey), these Pioneers look around and seek ways to improve where they are, where they came from, or where we all live together in the world. Philanthropy of this sort has the added advantage of educating the next generation in the values of the family, while teaching crucial skills for understanding and managing wealth.

THEY HELP THEIR PARENTS ADJUST

Remember, children in G2 are learning alongside their parents in the Land of Wealth. Many parents lag behind their children in adapting to wealth, or they fail to know what to teach. All too often, the children have to learn new skills and perspectives on their own. Just as immigrants have a reciprocal impact on the cultures they enter, children and grandchildren can have a reciprocal impact on parents and grandparents willing to listen, watch, and learn. The resilience, adaptability, and new experiences of G2 can influence how their parents acculturate to the family's adoptive land.

How Integration Benefits Estate Planning

Simply put, the strategy of Integration allows the greatest range of options for optimal estate planning with wealth. Where Avoidance and Assimilation each limit the opportunities for successful wealth transfers, Integration leads to a full range of possibilities based on estate size, G1's values and choices, and the degree to which G2 is prepared for handling wealth.

If G1 has had the wisdom to follow best practices in raising G2, the next generation will have a healthy balance between their middle-class heritage and the new legacy of responsible affluence. Estate planning choices will then be focused on individual issues within the family, based on the personality, values, capabilities, and needs of both G1 and G2.

Many of these choices again touch upon the core issue with wealth: complexity. Parents have to make complicated financial and estate-planning decisions about core questions, such as:

- How soon should I start transferring money to my children, balancing my needs and theirs?
- How do I decide whether to pass on wealth *equally to all* my children or *fairly to each* of my children?
- Should I pass on wealth directly, in trust, or some combination? If I use trusts, what is the best trust design? Do I use the same trust design for each of my children? Whom should I select as trustee?
- How do I balance passing on wealth to philanthropic causes, as well as to my heirs?

Keep in mind: 80 percent of those who live in the Land of Wealth have probably never had to deal with these issues before. These daunting dilemmas are all new and bewildering. The industries of estate planning, philanthropy, and wealth management stand at the ready with ideas and recommendations for these and related questions. But it is the successful acculturation of the family and its members that contributes to a good outcome, not just clever estate planning strategies that treat the money as the client.

———

Phil Spinelli knew his parents were incredibly proud of how he and Barb were handling their wealth so far. With prudent wealth management and reasonable spending, the Spinelli's assets continued to multiply beyond $50 million. But Phil wondered sometimes what his grandfather would think of his family's life. Although his grandfather had made his own leap from the Old Country to a middle-class version of the American Dream,

Phil's success was another magnitude up the scale. As the Spinellis met with their attorney to discuss plans for the children's trusts and for charitable gifting, Phil worried. Was he talking to his daughters enough about the family's roots, or having them see the lives of less fortunate people often enough? Were he and Barb using the money too often to make things easy?

In reality, Phil was doing fine. His occasional self-doubts kept him looking for opportunities to offset the tremendous pull of wealth. His image of his grandfather was like a compass in his heart, helping him and Barb keep the family on course through unfamiliar territory.

The Rewards of Integration

Pursuing a strategy of Integration offers wealth's Immigrants the opportunity to achieve the kind of balanced perspective most people would associate with solid, responsible living with wealth. At its best, it includes:

- Respect for the values of hard work, personal responsibility, and fairness.
- Pride in one's heritage, with a willingness to move among diverse social circles.
- Acceptance of being wealthy without guilt, shame, anxiety, or entitlement.
- A strong sense of family, one that recognizes and respects the hard work of elders, while simultaneously mentoring and supporting succeeding generations.
- Ability to work collaboratively with financial and legal advisors.
- Dedication to teaching children personal financial management and other life skills they will need to succeed.
- A sense of community responsibility and generosity of spirit.

From Acculturation to Adaptation

Thus far, we have examined the journey of immigration to wealth, discovering its amazing parallels to ethnic immigration and the life experience of those who move from one culture to another. We have used the research and theories of cross-cultural psychology to illuminate the strategies available to wealth's Immigrants as they try to adjust personally—to acculturate—to the paradise they find themselves in. We have seen that, just as with ethnic immigration, the strategies chosen start the family down paths that have far-reaching consequences.

Beginning with the personal journey of Immigration, passing through the gate of Acculturation, the family must now embark on the long road of Adaptation across generations. In the following section, we will examine the roadmap families can use as they make the transition from their working- or middle-class heritage to living successfully in the Land of Wealth. Once again, cross-cultural psychology will help guide the way. The culture, the tasks, and the challenges are, however, unique to wealth.

III

Adaptation

CHAPTER 8

From Acculturation to Adaptation

How wealth's Immigrants choose to acculturate sets the tone for how easily the family may adapt to the new economic culture in which it finds itself. The middle-class perspective and identity of G1 Immigrants must be transformed into the broader, more comprehensive perspective needed by G2s, G3s, and subsequent generations—*if* the family is to survive in the Land of Wealth. Though all wealth Immigrants may start off feeling like strangers in paradise, they must make their way toward being at ease in their new homeland by the third generation—or greatly risk G2's and G3's deportation.

The most favorable launching for the family occurs when wealth's newcomers in G1 are open to integrating elements of where they came from and where they now find themselves. If they reject any connection to wealth (as in the Avoidance strategy) or abandon the values of middle-class life (as in Assimilation), they will point the next generation down a lonely path without much guidance or preparation for handling affluence responsibly. G2 or G3 can still find their way back toward a balanced approach to handling wealth, but they will have to rely on themselves and other resources to do so.

———

A year after her divorce from Ted, Joan entertained her daughter Rachel, now in her mid-thirties, and Rachel's boyfriend, Jason, over Thanksgiving. Rachel was working with clients in the private banking department of a brokerage firm in Pittsburgh. Rachel and Jason, a trusts-and-estates attorney, were familiar with the world of wealth through their jobs, as well as friendships. At the dinner table, Rachel made reference to those who have much more than $10 million as having "real wealth." Jason agreed.

This touched a nerve with Joan. She accused her daughter of being spoiled. Rachel and Jason defended their view as simply true. They tried to explain that they live and work in a world where $10 million is entry-level wealth. This offended Joan, who had worked hard to become successful and manage what she had, despite the family turmoil. The words flung back and forth across the table would be familiar to any family of immigrants and natives: "You don't know how easy you have it!" and the retort: "You don't understand my situation; my life is different from yours. Life here is nothing like where you came from!" Joan felt her daughter was ungrateful, while Rachel saw her mother as out of touch. It took weeks for them to have a civil conversation about what had happened.

———

THE FAMILY'S ADAPTATION MUST ACCOMPLISH THREE MAIN GOALS: retain useful core elements of the middle-class perspective, shed extraneous or no-longer-relevant aspects, and add novel skills and understanding for the new environment. The bad news is that few in G1 know exactly what transformation must occur, what the steps entail, or how to accomplish them over time. The good news is that, after decades of progress in understanding the family dynamics of wealth, the steps are clear and the methods for accomplishing them are well defined.

The First Step: G1 to G2

Let's examine the pathway for family adaptation to wealth starting with the most common and straightforward situation, that of G1 Pioneers to wealth. We will follow these Immigrants as they face that core challenge: parenting their children in new, more affluent circumstances than they themselves experienced growing up.

TWO ASSUMPTIONS

To keep things simple, let's assume the family's investable net worth is near or within the high-net-worth (HNW) level of $5 million to $20 million. This level is enough to change the family's circumstances, but not so high that we need address issues more relevant for families in the ultra-high-net-worth (UHNW) range, well above $20 million. Factors at the UHNW level will be discussed in Chapter 10, when we examine families who must manage multiple generations with significant wealth.

A second assumption is that this discussion is based primarily on American perspectives about society and economic cultures. Middle-class attitudes in America are predominantly Western in nature. In other societies, with a much stronger orientation to family or clan, the transition from G1 to G2 and beyond is very different than what is described in this chapter and the next. Familial or collectivist cultures are characterized by a much more powerful focus on mutual dependence, shared assets, and a tribal mindset, compared to the individualistic focus characterizing Western middle-class culture. These familial cultures typically must adapt in the opposite direction as generations achieve wealth, developing more of a focus on independence and self-sufficiency in subsequent generations to balance the strong family orientation. All successful families around the globe must eventually build toward a balance of independence and interdependence. It is the starting point that differs.[76]

Building from One Perspective to Two

Figure 8-1 shows the initial steps in a family's adaptation to wealth, beginning with the transition from G1 to G2.

Many of wealth's Pioneers in G1 embark on their journey with a perspective firmly rooted in the beliefs and skills of successful middle-class entrepreneurs. They exalt those qualities associated with success: self-sufficiency, perseverance, a strong work ethic, independence, entrepreneurial orientation, ambition, individualism, and ability to delay gratification for future personal rewards. Of course, the entrepreneurial focus of some Pioneers is less individualistic and more collaborative; they possess additional skills and attitudes supporting leadership of teams in order to achieve business success. Yet, it is often the man or woman at the head of the business who maintains the vision, drive, and stamina to keep the business on track toward the Land of Wealth.

Arriving in economic paradise, G1 Immigrants embody these exalted middle-class qualities of independence, self-sufficiency, and initiative. As a result, they advocate for this perspective as the wellspring of

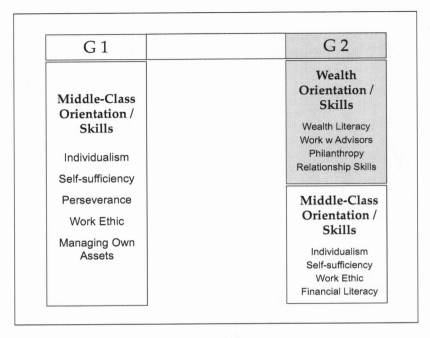

Figure 8-1: The initial transition between G1 and G2, building orienta-
tons and skills in G2 from the family's middle-class heritage and from the
new environment of wealth.

success. They also are likely to view these qualities as the keys to handling wealth. They are not altogether wrong; these qualities are necessary. They are simply not sufficient.

CARRYING OVER OLD VALUES AND SKILLS

Financially successful G1s naturally seek to foster these esteemed qualities in their children. They also may teach their children to be entrepreneurial, though they must remember that few people are disposed
to the stressful life of the entrepreneur. At the very least, benevolent
forward-thinking G1 parents try to mentor their children to possess
those core qualities from middle-class attitudes and skills (Figure 8-2).

These are the independence-oriented qualities and skills related to
individualism, self-sufficiency, work ethic, the capacity for good personal financial literacy, and the like.

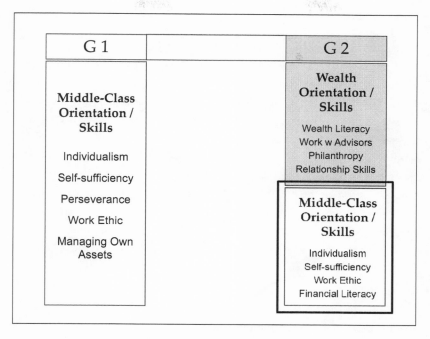

Figure 8-2: Some beneficial aspects of the middle-class orientation and skills parents need to foster in G2

Financial literacy education focuses partly on the core financial skills of life:[77]

- How to spend wisely in order to live within one's income.
- How to maintain and manage a savings reserve to minimize unexpected or large expenses impacting a regular budget.
- How to manage debt and credit responsibly.
- How to keep track of what one has (what comes in and what goes out) so effective adjustments can be made in a budget, as needed.
- How to manage one's assets, either by one's own efforts or through the appropriate use of financial advisors.

Good basic financial skills are important for anyone, rich or poor. But with wealth these become crucial. Otherwise the next generation quickly begins to lose its grounding in handling money at any level.

———

Max and Adrienne's son Adam celebrated turning sixteen with a big birthday bash at his house. With great fanfare, his parents led a blind-folded Adam to the driveway where a new silver BMW sat gleaming, a ribbon tied at the grille. He was ecstatic. He had been lobbying his par-ents for a new car for his birthday for a long time. Now it was his.

Later at the party, friends peppered him with questions: How fast would it go? Could they get a ride in it? What did he think it cost? On the patio by the pool, one of his friends (the daughter of a local banker who was educating her on spending and saving) asked Adam a very different question: How much did he think the insurance was going to cost? Adam laughed and shrugged his shoulders. "I have absolutely no idea. Who cares? I'm not paying for it!" The girl smiled but inside, she thought, "Oh, boy. Trouble."

———

INSTILLING NEW VALUES AND SKILLS

As G1 parents soon learn, middle-class values, skills, and identity are helpful but not sufficient when living with wealth. New skills, attitudes, and perspectives are required and must become part of G2's develop-ment as well. So, intelligent and adaptive G1s must foster a second layer of skills and perspectives in the children growing up Native to wealth.

G1s must work to instill in their children what may be called a *wealth orientation and set of skills* (Figure 8-3). This is a parallel process to how G1s must integrate the old and the new in their own accultur-ation to wealth.

New skills include some or all of the following:

- Working with Advisors: Understanding how one's wealth is man-aged, by whom, and within what basic parameters; being able to collaborate and share in decision-making with one's advisors, rang-ing from attorneys to wealth managers to philanthropic advisors.

- Working with Trusts: Understanding and working well with trust-ees as an educated and responsible beneficiary; being aware of the provisions of one's trust(s); living within the parameters of

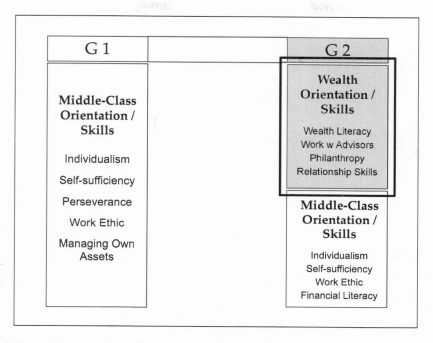

Figure 8-3: Some beneficial aspects of the wealth orientation and skills parents need to foster in G2.

how income and principal distributions occur; understanding and learning the responsibilities of eventually becoming a co-trustee, if possible under the terms of the trust.

- **Communication and Wealth Identity:** Being able to talk about wealth in close relationships and to communicate within the family about wealth matters; achieving a sense of comfort with wealth, i.e., having a sense of identity alongside, but separate from, one's identity as a person of wealth; having skills for managing the complexities of relationships with others who are not wealthy.

- **Having and Acting with Purpose:** devoting oneself to some purposeful activity (whether in paid work or unpaid activity) with perseverance, dedication, and satisfaction.

- **Sharing the Wealth:** Understanding and implementing philanthropic activities either alone or together with other members of

the family; making decisions about charitable giving using modern methods of grant-making or philanthropy; being purposeful
rather than reflexive in using wealth for social causes.

Developing this new orientation occurs through a process involving
many activities: family communication, financial education, discussion of values, love, and a judicious use of limit-setting and enforcement of consequences.

Effective G1 parents foster good decision-making so their children
are able to manage larger amounts of money than their parents encountered at the same age. The children are also gradually introduced in
adolescence or adulthood to trusted family advisors, including financial
advisors, attorneys, accountants, and others. Because the family typically learns to talk about issues openly, there is early and timely discussion about dealing with the various stresses of being wealthy. These
range from relationship complexities to staying grounded as a fortunate individual in a society where many people struggle with not having
basic necessities of life. All of these contribute a general development
of what is termed a healthy *wealth identity:* the psychological and social
attitudes underpinning good (not inflated) self-esteem, lack of guilt or
shame, and self-confidence about handling wealth productively.

Gina Spinelli was truly her father's daughter. She had a head for business
ever since she ran her first lemonade stand at age ten. She grew up when
the family was still largely middle class, and she had built a solid work
ethic and sense of initiative as a result.

After earning an undergrad degree in business and then an MBA,
Gina was working for an aircraft-leasing company when Phil's liquidity
event occurred. She was happy for him and fascinated by the whole process, including the wealth management needed to protect and grow the
money. Phil and Barb decided to include Gina when they interviewed
high-end financial firms and attorneys. She stayed in the background but
seemed to absorb everything.

For his part, Phil completed his one-year transition at SteriMetrix, did part-time consulting for about six months, and then began to
look around for his next career project. By then, Gina had five years of

business experience in the aircraft leasing company, including being mentored by a firm but supportive boss. When Phil had the opportunity to invest in a struggling manufacturer with a diverse line of industrial filtration devices, he approached Gina to see if she would be willing to work in the business. They talked over the pros and cons of working together as a family business. They decided to try.

The Role of Family Meetings

One of the most important actions a family of wealth can perform is to institute a process of family communication, including regular family meetings. Family meetings are excellent vehicles for passing on values, educating family members about finances and other topics, modeling the ability to communicate, and providing a fail-safe mechanism for times of stress, conflict, or crisis.

Family meetings tend to be a rare event for most families of wealth, as they are for families in general. Some reasons carry forward from working- or middle-class life. Few families hold even informal meetings on any regular basis, other than talking about family issues during meals. (Gathering for meals itself has become a vanishing activity in the modern world.) When families migrate to the Land of Wealth, they carry over their prior lack of regular communication as a family. So, there is little tradition to build upon.

Even those families who do have a history of communicating may be reluctant to begin including discussions about their wealth. Society's well-known taboos around discussing money, let alone wealth, come into play here. Furthermore, as mentioned throughout this book, most economic Immigrants have no template to work from in understanding how to talk about wealth. And most newly wealthy families are under the impression that talking about wealth will be the worst thing to do, not the best. "Don't let the kids know the family is rich" is the widely held belief. So families either don't know how to talk about wealth, don't want to talk about wealth, or are afraid to talk about wealth.

The reality is that a skillful process of communicating about money, values, and events in the family dramatically improves the odds of

success across generations. This is so fundamental it cannot be emphasized enough. The first step, then, is for families to get past their skepticism about communication, whether casually in daily life or more
formally in a family meeting process.

Appendix III discusses how families can organize and conduct family meetings. This overview includes a set of well-developed ground
rules for family communication. These may be very helpful for families
unused to sharing thoughts and reactions openly or safely.

Fostering the Two Layers

The triad of methods for teaching about wealth—family communication, the passing on of values along with the money, and the preparation of heirs via financial education and training—must be added to
the core strengths of a middle-class orientation and values. Many of
these extra factors are not unique to being affluent. Financial literacy,
devotion to charitable giving, and grounded self-esteem are a part of
any responsible and socially aware life. But they are critical for handling even a modest amount of wealth. They also lay the groundwork
for passing on these values and skills to the next generation.

In this first transition for the family new to the Land of Wealth,
developing the next generation feels like a layering-on of skills rather
than a naturally integrated way of parenting. It grows from the layering-on of new behaviors and attitudes occurring as parents adjust to
wealth themselves. These dual orientations need to be taught by G1
parents who only recently migrated from middle-class life. Fostering
strong, capable, well-grounded children with wealth is far from obvious to the Immigrant whose own identity was forged in the middle-class
or blue-collar world. For all but the most adept and insightful parents,
bringing up G2 in the new environment will have its fits and starts, its
guesses, and its setbacks. G1s are still feeling their own way with wealth.
They are unlikely to know all that needs to be concurrently done with
G2—but they must try.

Phil and Barb's daughter Stephanie began her campaign to get a car at age sixteen. Barb, who had had to take buses until halfway through college, didn't think there was a need for a car at Stephanie's age, no matter how much money the family now had. Phil was more willing to listen. He persuaded Barb they could use this as an opportunity to teach Stephanie some important basics about self-responsibility and finance.

First, Phil and Barb insisted the vehicle had to be a used but reliable make and model, at least four years old. They wanted Stephanie to have the experience of taking care of a car that needed occasional maintenance. They required she research which models were more dependable. They introduced her to their local mechanic who showed Stephanie the fundamentals of checking the oil, tire pressures, coolant levels, and the like. They set a budget consistent with a moderately priced used car, including figuring how much of Stephanie's savings to use for the purchase and the costs of registering and insuring the car. She had been given an allowance since age eight and had built up savings over the years from gifts, babysitting jobs, and doing extra chores around the house.

The family spent two months driving various vehicles to get a feel for what was available. In the end, Stephanie chose a black pickup truck with low mileage at a good price. Phil and Barb allowed her one extravagance: a vanity plate that said TRUK-GRL.

Preparing to Receive Wealth

Building the dual orientations of middle-class culture and wealth culture is important for more than just teaching G2s to take care of themselves in adult life. G2s will also need to be prepared to manage whatever personal assets are passed on to them, outright or as beneficiaries of trusts. As shown in Figure 8-4, G2s properly prepared for an affluent adult life will be able to receive whatever wealth is transferred to them, while their parents are alive or through inheritance.

When G2 is prepared with a thoughtful blend of middle-class skills and values, plus new skills for being affluent, wealth transferred from one generation to the next is handled more successfully. G1 is able to

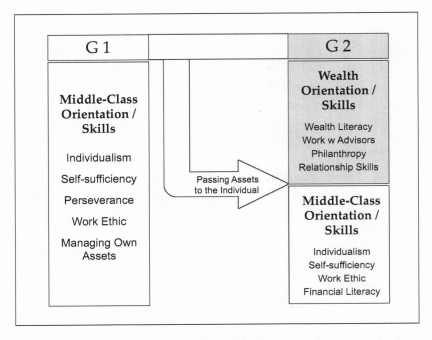

Figure 8-4: Properly prepared adult children in G2 are able to handle assets passed on to them outright or in trust.

help through annual gifting, financial assistance with down payments on homes, seed money for starting businesses or new careers, or opening of new investment accounts to be owned by the next generation. Eventually, wealth transferred through inheritance is more successful and less stressful when adult children are prepared to receive their portion of their parents' estates responsibly. Even if G1 chooses to pass on assets in trust for estate or tax planning purposes, G2 is still prepared to be good beneficiaries and to work effectively with trustees, using good personal financial self-management.

———

The Spinellis discussed how to plan and pay for Stephanie's college education. Although Phil and Barb could use the easy, tax-advantaged method of paying educational expenses directly to the institution from their own money, they decided to fund a Uniform Gift to Minors

(UGMA) account of several hundred thousand dollars. Phil was the trustee-like custodian of the account, alongside Stephanie as the minor (under age twenty-one) account holder. They knew whatever money left in the account would be hers to use when she turned twenty-one, with the risk she would spend it frivolously. But they wanted to use this account as financial training wheels to teach her skills for her future adult life with wealth.

Phil explained to Stephanie how the UGMA account worked, how to read the investment account statements, and how check writing occurred for tuition, books, and other expenses. When she came home from college for weekends or vacations, he and Stephanie sat together and wrote out the checks for his signature. The first time she wrote a big check for tuition she was shocked at the amount. It gave her an appreciation of the costs of college in a very tangible way. By the time she turned twenty-one and the UGMA account became hers to manage, she was relatively adept at reading financial statements and managing thousands of dollars. The transition was seamless and steady.

———

ALL TOO QUICKLY AFTER LANDING IN PARADISE, G1 MUST BE LOOKing ahead to what their children in G2 will need to learn in adult life, as Natives in the Land of Wealth. G1 must start noticing and identifying teachable moments to instill this blend of middle-class culture and wealth in order to create success for their children, and ultimately for the family.

When the Transition Falters

Unfortunately, too few parents are able to build even some of the competencies needed by their children to handle life with wealth. In the grind of everyday life—and without a roadmap to point the way—many G1s neglect the active teaching of these skills. This leaves G2 vulnerable to being raised with affluence without the beliefs and behaviors necessary for success. Figure 8-5 shows the all-too-typical case for families newly arrived in paradise: a lack of preparation for the full range of skills and perspectives needed to handle the family's new circumstances.

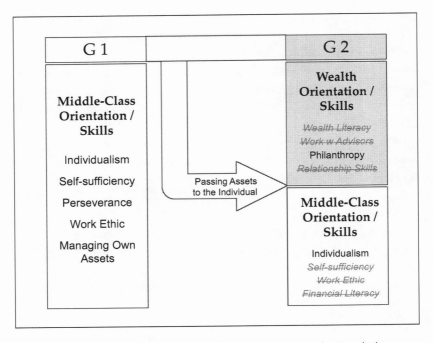

Figure 8-5: When G2 is unprepared with the competencies needed to handle assets passed on to them by G1.

The crossed-out skills in Figure 8-5 represent the absent or under-developed competencies that leave G2 unprepared for life with afflu-ence. G1 parents may pass on some qualities, such as an inclination for independence, by simply using exhortations to "be a strong successful individual." Perhaps the parents teach a little about philanthropy. But the necessary grounding in financial literacy, work ethic, self-sufficiency, and healthy self-esteem may be partially or wholly absent. Children in G2 are left without adequate preparation for either middle-class life or life with wealth, a truly unfortunate situation.

Compounding the problem is that assets may eventually be passed to the next generation, either during the parents' lives or upon inher-itance. The capacity to handle these assets, however, will have gaping holes where important skills should be present. And in a self-fulfill-ing cycle, if parents decide their children are not capable of handling money, then the inheritance either goes elsewhere (to philanthropy, perhaps) or gets locked up in trust with strict provisions under the control of trustees.

At this crucial first transition from G1 to G2, failure to combine the core skills of successful middle-class life with good preparation for affluence begins to erode the family's chances for adaptation to their new economic culture. This lack of perspective and abilities leaves the family susceptible to the unchecked power of wealth, to relationship stresses, and to corrosive influences on identity and self-esteem.

——

The Morgan's eldest daughter Alicia was an attractive young woman who worked hard, saved her money, and enjoyed her job as a pharmacist. The problem was that her relationships with men rarely lasted more than a year or two. She had a deep aversion to boyfriends' spending money on her, and she had a hard time spending money on herself.

When dates bought Alicia flowers, she'd say they didn't really need to —and she meant it. A nice night on the town made her uncomfortable. When a young man she was dating got a long-overdue promotion and drove up proudly in a used Corvette he had just bought, she told him she "hated guys who show off." Her relationships usually deteriorated when the men realized that they couldn't enjoy occasionally splurging on her, or with her. They also learned she avoided bringing anyone to meet her parents.

One day, while looking for stamps, Alicia's current boyfriend stumbled across a stack of unopened envelopes in the top drawer of her desk at home. When he asked her about them, Alicia said some contained checks from her parents or their advisors; the rest were investment statements. She didn't want to deal with it, and she didn't want to talk about it. She associated the money with guilt, shame, and anger at how her parents were living with wealth. But she also didn't know what to do with her feelings. That part of her life felt stuck.

——

The Second Step: G2 to G3

If the family has been successful in that first fragile transition from G1 to G2, the next step is the transition from G2 to G3. This transition is aimed at furthering the integration of wealth skills with what were originally the grounded and productive aspects of the middle-class perspective. (Figure 8-6).

If the family successfully gains familiarity with affluence, the dual orientations fostered in G2 lay the groundwork for raising G3 with a fuller, more integrated approach to wealth. What was difficult and strange for G1 to accomplish may now be synthesized for G3 into a more natural capacity for handling personal life with wealth.

—

The Spinellis celebrated the arrival of their first grandchild with great joy. Gina had married William, a wonderfully down-to-earth man and a fourth-generation heir in a St. Louis family worth $450 million. Most of their friends assumed they were just two wealthy heirs with similar backgrounds. Yet Gina and William recognized the differences in how they grew up and how they felt navigating in the world of wealth. He had

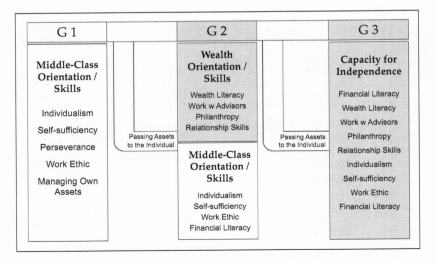

Figure 8-6: Building the capacity for independence for G3

known nothing else, while Gina still felt like a newcomer sometimes. She was surprised to find herself feeling intimidated when visiting his family, even though they were more than welcoming. Next to their wealth, Gina's family's resources—now grown to over $60 million—seemed small.

Phil and Barb felt much the same way. Barb held Gina's baby in her arms and thought, this child will only know a life of wealth. The family's lower-middle-class roots will be long past. It had been one thing to teach Gina and Stephanie about handling the jump to affluence. It felt entirely different to imagine raising this new little grandchild with anything familiar from Barb's own background. She wasn't sure how she could keep the best aspects of their former life part of this precious girl's new life.

———

FOR G3, THE FAMILY'S HERITAGE NOW CONTAINS ELEMENTS FROM two economic cultures, not one. The residue of G1's Immigrant perspective—take care of your own life, be independent, be self-sufficient, have a good work ethic, manage whatever assets you have in a prudent and responsible fashion—lives on, supporting the grandchildren's integrated functioning and values. In addition, from early childhood on, G3 is afforded opportunities to learn the additional set of skills, values, and perspectives needed to live capably in the world of affluence they inhabit:

- Parents and grandparents can proactively teach the next generation how to work with the family's advisors.
- G3s can identify themselves as Natives of wealth in a grounded, natural manner.
- G3s can learn skills for communicating about wealth within the family and in close relationships.
- G3s can understand and participate in philanthropic activities with humility and passion.

In this admittedly optimistic but not unrealistic scenario, G3s are prepared to handle themselves as individuals in the Land of Wealth. No longer identifying with the middle class yet respecting and maintaining the solid values passed on from their Immigrant forebears, they truly have the best of both worlds. What they have developed is an integrated *capacity for independence* in life, a remarkable set of skills and perspectives that society doesn't normally associate with grandchildren of wealth creators.[78]

Understanding the Capacity for Independence

It is hard for most G1 wealth-creators to grasp the unique nature of the adaptation process required to foster down-to-earth, successful G2s and G3s. When I've described this goal to G1s, for example, they sometimes scoff at how any trust beneficiary could truly have a "capacity for independence" when relying on trust income for even a portion of their financial life. They argue that no one is truly independent who counts on trust income or distributions. G1s' zeroing in on this aspect is a reflection of how they see the world. They benchmark independence to whether someone is *financially* independent, rather than seeing the bigger picture of how someone manages their life. They equate independence with financial self-sufficiency, one of those hallmarks of the entrepreneurial Pioneer.

The "capacity for independence" for Natives of wealth is a broad description of how someone conducts themselves financially, emotionally, and in relationships. A G3 who is financially literate, spends within their income, manages credit and debt well, has purpose and a work ethic, and can adapt to changes in economic circumstances functions as an independent person, whether or not trust income happens to be part of their financial support. It is akin to the middle-class person who lives prudently within a salary and, if that salary disappears in a layoff, has the personal and financial resources to survive and find another job. Most G3s with a well-developed capacity for independence have paid jobs in addition to any trust income, because they like to work and they want to earn their own money. They wisely see their trust income as one income source among many.

Beyond the financial aspect, however, the capacity of independence involves many qualities. It means a person has a strong sense of identity, self-esteem, and adaptability. They are neither passive and dependent in relationships nor overly controlling and self-centered. They know who they are and what they have to offer the world, apart from their wealth yet utilizing their wealth. They have a capacity to think, act, feel, and support themselves independently because they have been raised to be resilient, capable, and financially savvy. They also learn skills for managing the power of wealth and the complexities of living among a diverse group of economic classes and cultures.

GRAPPLING WITH THE POWER OF WEALTH

Balancing the power that society accords money requires a strong spirit and a centered personality. As the statesman Edmund Burke wrote, "If we command our wealth, we shall be rich and free. If our wealth commands us, we are poor indeed."

One of the most difficult tasks parents face in the Land of Wealth is how to foster personality development capable of withstanding—let alone harnessing—the tremendous power society grants to wealth. Many economic Immigrants struggle to do this effectively, never having experienced the power of wealth before and never having been taught how to handle the power of wealth in balanced ways. The three core processes that create healthy offspring—teaching of values, preparation via skill development, and open family communication—are the ways to avoid creating inheritors who run rampant with wealth or are crushed by it to become passive, dependent, and weak. The processes help form the foundation for that capacity for independence required of each generation with wealth.

BEING WEALTHY IN A NON-WEALTHY SOCIETY

"Living in the Land of Wealth" is quite literal for some ultra-high-net-worth (UHNW) families. It is not a metaphor. They inhabit, socialize, engage in activities with, and rarely venture beyond enclaves of the very wealthy. But for most high-net-worth (HNW) families and even some UHNW families, the Land of Wealth is largely metaphorical. They still live their lives among and around regular middle-class people, within a middle-class culture.

Remember that those possessing over $1 million in investable net worth represent about 8 percent of US households, and those with $9 million or more represent only 1 percent. Viewed strictly through the math of demographics, this means Immigrants to wealth from middle-class life migrate from being part of a majority culture to being a member of a very tiny minority. Natives are born into this minority culture. Because of this, Natives need family support to provide guidance and help them respond to what is traditionally labeled as "cross-class stresses."

The hostile envy of society toward the wealthy gives rise to mixed messages about "The Rich" as a minority. Since most people view wealth as envious, its minority status is therefore considered elite (becoming part of that elite is what drives some to immigrate to the Land of Wealth in the first place). Few recognize that the wealthy encounter stereotyping as part of their minority status. Fewer still have any sympathy for this experience.

———

The years went by and Max and Adrienne's son Alex was well into his second marriage, with a daughter, Rosemary, reaching college age. Rosemary had grown up with an affluent lifestyle due to the very generous (and ongoing) support of her grandparents, the Morgans. As a freshman, Rosemary moved into her dormitory at a mid-tier liberal arts college. Her clothes, shoes, room decorations, and technology devices shouted "Rich Girl" to everyone . . . except her. When a student journalist from the campus website came around to interview new students and photograph their rooms, Rosemary chatted away about her choice of decorations, glad to be of help.

When the article was posted, Rosemary was shocked to discover how opulent her room appeared to the working-class journalist—and to most of the campus. She was equally stunned to see how the journalist portrayed what seemed like Rosemary's cluelessness about her fellow classmates' more modest circumstances.

The ensuing fallout was even more instructive. Rosemary became the target of nasty online comments about the wealthy. She also became an object of desire by others, a target for being hit up for loans by some, and someone who was expected to pay for every drink or meal when out with others. Back home for the holidays, her parents berated her for having permitted the interview in the first place. "What were you thinking?" they admonished. "Didn't you know how people would respond?" She didn't.

ECONOMIC IMMIGRANTS NEED TO TEACH THEIR CHILDREN HOW to respond when confronted with social attitudes about those who have or inherit wealth. These skills include knowing how to be sensitive to situations of economic diversity, how to make decisions whether to engage with or to step away from situations reflecting stereotyping, and how to be assertive in facing social attitudes or stigmas associated with being wealthy.

The answers lie in G1s' talking early and often to children and grand-children about these issues, recognizing and using teachable moments within their everyday life or in family meetings. Parents need to talk about what wealth can and cannot do, about being humble yet appre-ciative of success, about pride and responsibility for having more than enough to live on. The difficult part is to convey the complexities about being wealthy without building in mistrust, resentment about being stereotyped, or undue pride about the family's status. It is this need for balance, nuance, complexity, and support that is so hard when par-ents haven't come from wealth themselves. However, their children and grandchildren are counting on them to pass on those skills.

Those who come to wealth need an understanding of the life skills their children and grandchildren will need in order to manage the complexity of living *within* the majority culture, while not being *of* the majority culture.

Building Skills on their Own

What happens when G2 and G3 are not well prepared by G1 to han-dle the complexities of wealth? Unfortunately, for all the reasons out-lined in this book, that is the norm. Can the next generation find ways to build their own understanding and skills for wealth?

The answer is yes. Many G2s and G3s find their own ways toward a healthy, balanced capacity for independence, despite their lack of preparation or even a mishandling of parental training. They do so through pursuing various means of personal growth and development, outside the family.

Some Natives of paradise learn about handling wealth through reading. Wealth counselors experienced in coaching inheritors have written
excellent books over the past twenty years about how to resolve feelings of guilt, passivity, dependency, or entitlement.[79] Next-generation
members of family businesses—the main method by which significant
wealth is accumulated—have a raft of books and articles available on
how to navigate the complexities of families in business.

Some inheritors find support and guidance through therapy, whether
through standard routes or from therapists with special training around
issues of money and wealth.[80]

Other G2s and G3s find tremendous benefit from peer resources
and organizations, learning from each other and from experts about the
very skills outlined in this book.[81] Once G2s or G3s have tapped into
these networks, they are often able to access the entire set of resources
—books, experts, therapists, and organizations—that may guide them
to what they need for prospering with wealth. There are many avenues
available to fill in those gaps in skills and understanding left vacant by
parents understandably unprepared for the task.

Dennis Jaffe has pointed out that the next generation's journey to
develop purpose and identity on their own is often a necessary part of
breaking away from the family, to finding their own way.[82] G2s and G3s
must build out their understanding of wealth, their place in the family enterprise, and their purpose in the world as fortunate individuals,
apart from the influences of parents and grandparents. Once G2s and
G3s have started to achieve their individual identities, anchored in the
unique circumstances of their lives as Natives of wealth, they then can
reconnect with G1s on a more equal footing.

Parenting the Parents

Fostering skills for wealth isn't necessarily a one-way process from parent to child. A wonderful outcome of the next generation's growth
occurs when G2 or G3 turns and helps G1 adjust to wealth in a healthier manner. Just as immigrants to a new culture act on that culture
to change it, new skills and perspectives by G2 and G3 can enhance
how G1 copes as well. As G2s and G3s learn new strategies, make new

connections, and break free from their challenges with wealth, they often try to bring these changes to parents who may have encountered an impasse in their own adjustment. That is why, in the roadmap of adaptation across generations (Figure 8-6), the bars connecting G1, G2, and G3 are not directional. The learning can go both ways.

Just the Beginning

The elements discussed so far transfer the best of middle-class life to living with wealth. With focused, thoughtful parenting and wise understanding of the adaptations needed for wealth, development of well-rounded G2s lays the groundwork for further refinement and adaptation for G3—and hopefully G4. If G2 or G3 inherits assets only in their own name or as beneficiaries of trusts, the capacity for independence is all that is required.

This set of transitions is also sufficient if the assets of the family are passed on in small enough divisions so the amount each individual owns is at a more modest economic level. In other words, when the family's large reservoir of water is divided into individual tanks and given to each heir for their own use, the generations move on independently. Those Natives in G3 may have been raised with affluence, but the assets themselves may be diminished due to the effects of taxes, normal spending, too many family members, and the vagaries of economic cycles. G3s must then either replenish their own wealth or accept that they must live on less as middle-class individuals.

But what if successive generations must continue to draw from a common reservoir? What if their reserves remain commingled, due to economies of scale, estate planning, tax benefits, or other good reasons? This communal transfer of the family's reserves is rare in middle-class life, but common in modern wealth. Developing the capacity for independence is then only half the story. For greater levels of wealth, handed down from one generation to the next as shared assets, another set of skills and perspectives must be fostered within the family.

CHAPTER 9

Learning to Function as a Family

M iddle-class families don't often own shared assets. Parents have their own checking, savings, or retirement accounts, which they rarely discuss. Children have theirs, which they rarely discuss. Adult brothers and sisters earn and manage their own finances.

There are exceptions, of course. Some farm families share land ownership. Many family businesses grant ownership shares to multiple family members. Interestingly, working-class life actually has more community- and family-oriented attitudes and activities than middle-class life does. This is driven by the necessity to band together and care for each other in the face of severe adversity and scarcity.[83] At the middle-class level, though, shared assets are few and reasons or opportunities to make financial decisions together are infrequent.

Embracing the Family Enterprise

Some families in paradise are fortunate enough to sidestep wealth's many landmines to reach a very high level of success. These families typically begin with a family business or operating company that flourishes well beyond successful middle-class families. This typically occurs in the ultra-high-net-worth (UHNW) level well north of $50 million, up into the realm of $100 million to billions of dollars.

Families who share a large business or who work together with intricate structures of wealth function in what is called a *family enterprise*. Their financial, legal, and personal lives are intertwined in some or all of the following complex activities:

- One or more core businesses or operating companies.
- Real estate holdings.

- Investments in various markets around the world, including ownership of commodities, such as precious metals or timber.
- Trusts, financial partnerships, and other entities set up for business, tax, insurance, or estate planning purposes.
- Income generated via dividends, bonds, distributions from partnerships and trusts, or real estate investments.
- One or more family foundations and various social and community philanthropic activities.
- Ownership and management of domestic and international residences and vacation properties.
- Ownership of yachts, art collections, expensive vehicles, wine cellars, and other collectible or hard assets.

These assets and entities are particularly important by the time the third generation develops. Shared assets must be passed on or held in trust for inheritors who may not have been around when the family's outpost in the Land of Wealth was originally created.

The complexity of shared wealth changes a family significantly. They have to make decisions and interact with each other on a more complicated level than as a regular family or even as a small family business. The next important set of adaptations that must occur for these families is a transformation in their methods and skills for leadership and decision-making.

Family Perspective, Family Skills

To handle this added level of complexity and shared responsibility, a new set of skills and perspectives must be fostered starting at G2 or G3, depending on when the shared assets begin to occur. A *family* perspective must be created, over and above the individually focused skills and attitudes of the family founders. The family then has to develop skills for collaborating, making decisions, and sharing without descending into conflict.

This is hard. As Susan, an exasperated G2 in a wealthy family once put it: "Growing up, we couldn't even figure out how to share what was in the beach house refrigerator without getting into fights. How were we going to be able to share the *beach house* without killing each other?!"

Having large amounts of money or ownership assets in common with other people is, from a middle-class model of individualism, a disaster waiting to happen. Unless families receive preparation for the difficult task of sharing assets, Natives of wealth can slide into family squabbling that will eventually lead to dissolution of the assets and possibly of the family itself.

The Capacity for Interdependence

Preparation for managing shared assets together begins with the development of a family orientation to wealth, accompanied by new skills not typically utilized in middle-class life. These skills and perspectives foster a *capacity for interdependence* for Natives of wealth. This capacity must be added to, and in balance with, the capacity for independence described in the previous chapter.

A well-formed capacity for interdependence embodies attitudes, behaviors, identity, and skills focused on how the family functions together in healthy ways. It captures a sense of belonging, family identity, pride in the family legacy, and loyalty to the family tribe. It embodies skills for negotiating and making decisions together through informal or formal structures that govern the extended family (what is called *governance* in the family wealth/family business world). It promotes a desire to be good stewards of the family enterprise and its wealth for the benefit of present and future generations, not just for the individual.

The top section of Figure 9-1 summarizes a few of these additional skills constituting the capacity for interdependence for members of G2, G3, and beyond.

For the families who adapt successfully to wealth across generations, the layered-on cultures of G2 are transformed to the fully integrated nature of G3. The third generation, no longer arising from middle-class culture, must harbor within themselves the DNA of their middle-class forebears, alongside a new cultural understanding of wealth. Capacities for both *independent* living and *interdependent* living must co-exist

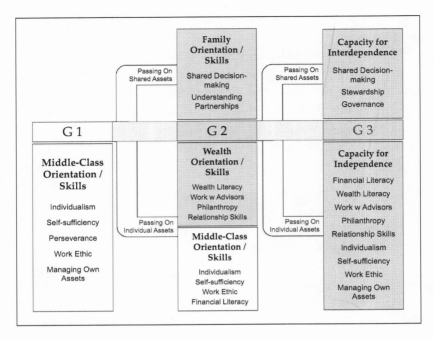

Figure 9-1: Adaptations of the family across generations necessary for handling personal and shared wealth.

and complement each other for success in the higher reaches of wealth. When they do, the individual and the family both benefit.[84]

––––

Ever since Stephanie had finished high school, the Spinellis had begun having regular family meetings once a year around the July 4th holiday. They would gather at their summer home in Maine for at least two days. For a half a day or more, they'd sit together in the living room to go over what was happening with the family, its finances, and any information or decisions that had to be discussed. Phil and Barb had shared the family's finances with both children completely, including any plans about estate planning, trusts, anticipated purchases, or the advisors they were using. Early on, they had to be patient with Stephanie's tendency to jump to solutions without thinking, or Gina's surprising reluctance to do anything that held risk. They also had to restrain themselves from offering the solution to every problem.

Over time, the Spinellis watched their children learn to balance each other and grow into decision-making. When Gina's husband William joined the family, he fit right in as an active contributor. A turning point occurred when a piece of property came on the market next to their summerhouse. Phil and Barb let the next generation take the lead in researching its investment potential, in conjunction with their wealth management team. The decision was made to proceed. They all began to operate together as a team, and over the following years they made many such decisions together.

———

The Difficult Road to Collaboration

Some middle-class families foster skills for collaboration—extended families with a strong sense of community, farm families owning property shared with other family branches, and families of faith whose values and history include shared decision-making. Yet in most middle-class families, shared decision-making is under-developed or absent. This is especially true in those families devoted to the individualism and independence that sprout Pioneers.

WHEN THE OUTPOST BECOMES A METROPOLIS

To understand the natural transitions leading to interdependence, let's return to the metaphor of the Pioneer entrepreneur who makes the journey to a new land and establishes an outpost there for his or her family. During the lifetime of the founder, the outpost grows, becoming increasingly prosperous and self-sustaining. The wealth-creating patriarch or matriarch leads the family, typically using a top-down leadership model in which he or she retains veto control over decision-making.

When the children reach adulthood, the Pioneer *may* seek their opinion, but their input is usually viewed as a voice, not a vote. As G2s mature, they *might* be awarded greater input on decisions about the family, the business, or perhaps even its wealth management. They might be asked to weigh in on decisions about shared assets, such as a family vacation home. If a member of the next generation shows promise or interest, the issue of succession emerges regarding the family's wealth or the business driving the family's wealth.

But much like a city that grows without professional planning or government, the family awakens one day to find themselves overwhelmed by the complexity of their financial and business circumstances. They face inefficiencies resulting from lack of foresight or knowledgeable administration. They must contend with the aging of the founding entrepreneur, his autonomous decision-making approach, and his personal notions about running the overall enterprise with its many parts and functions.

The once-small outpost has become an enterprise—one that must shift into stable, long-term management, with as much emphasis on efficiency and productivity as on growth and expansion. Yet, few G1 entrepreneurs know how to make this shift from the excitement of establishing outposts to the efficiency of running mature family enterprises.

FAMILY BONDS: SHACKLES OR SECURITY?

For many G1s, collaboration feels unnecessary, or even a curse. The need for G2 and G3 to learn healthy *inter*dependence is a mystery to these founding Immigrants. Shared assets are perceived from their middle-class perspective as shackles hobbling the pursuit of personal happiness and success. They believe it is simpler and easier just to manage whatever you own by yourself.

With fierce independence as their banner, G1s think that preparing heirs for shared decision-making is folly. Whatever decision-making has to be done should be accomplished either by one strong leader or by professional advisors who do this for a living. There is no expectation that yet-to-be-born grandchildren could ever be trusted to manage a family enterprise. Wealth-creators and their advisors plan for the family's management to be delegated to trained professionals. The assumption is that G2s and G3s will not know how to do so.

In a self-fulfilling prophecy, these intransigent Pioneers hold onto the reins of decision-making as long as possible, managing the family enterprise with a firm grip, failing (or even refusing) to understand how succeeding generations could be taught to work together.

FAMILY GOVERNANCE AS A MYSTERY

Much like the lack of knowledge about family adaptation, ignorance of the need for family governance is the norm rather than the exception for these Pioneer Immigrants. They struggle to understand how interdependence and collaborative leadership can enhance rather than inhibit the development of succeeding generations.

These clients are mystified when family wealth advisors broach the idea of shared governance and other family-focused activities. They may be willing to listen to the importance of philanthropy as a means to contribute to society, or to teach the next generation how to manage money. But they cling to their trust in individualism and personal initiative. Meanwhile, work proceeds apace on the many financial, legal, tax, and estate planning strategies that pass on the family's wealth to G2s and G3s, whether or not these generations are prepared to receive the assets. There is no attempt to foster the skills of shared decision-making in succeeding generations.

The result has several risks. It can produce passive, dependent "trust fund babies" unable to function outside the family's ongoing financial support, led by advisors and one or two family members. These heirs lack skills for understanding or managing the family's collective wealth. Or, it can over-emphasize strong-minded individualists unable to make decisions together, leading to rifts and internecine battles for control of the wealth.

Coming out of their heritage middle-class culture, G1 Pioneers don't realize that their children and grandchildren need to be prepared to handle wealth themselves *and* to work collaboratively if estate planning creates shared assets. So the preparation is never planned and never occurs. For many Immigrants to wealth, it seems wiser to simply deport the next generation back to middle-class life and let them build their own outposts.

This lack of preparation for governance and interdependence is a major contributor to the shirtsleeves-to-shirtsleeves pattern.

———

Max and Adrienne had real problems on their hands as they headed into their early eighties. Their eldest daughter Alicia visited only rarely with her husband and two children, though the Morgans weren't altogether unhappy with that. They found her difficult to deal with. Their middle son Alex had tried his hand at a series of poorly planned and poorly managed businesses that constantly required capital to stay afloat. He was also on his third marriage, with his first two wives receiving big portions of his wealth and generous alimony payments. He had always somehow neglected to finish the prenuptial agreements his parents and advisors had strongly advised. His four kids from three marriages seemed to struggle through whatever stage of life they were in.

The Morgans' youngest, Adam, had been their hope but now seemed to be following in his brother's footsteps. He had never finished his undergraduate degree, due to poor grades and frequent absences. He worked as a guide doing mountain climbing. The biggest concern was that his ego seemed as monumental as some of the peaks he scaled. He always had grandiose plans that never seemed to pan out. On top of everything, Max and Adrienne were concerned about their own wealth, which had been depleted by years of mismanagement, overspending, and support of the next generation.

———

When Immigrant Skills Get Dissipated

Figure 9-2 shows the unfortunate situation where assets are being passed along but there are major gaps in G2 or G3's skills for receiving these assets. The crossed-out areas again represent the missing or underdeveloped skills needed either for independence at the personal level or interdependence at the family level.

Without guidance, wealth's Natives become strangers in the paradise that should be their homeland. Although they receive or benefit from the family's wealth, they develop few skills for competently navigating their lives, financially or otherwise.

There is an interesting parallel to this process related to ethnic immigrant families adapting to American life. The *immigrant paradox*[85] is "a pattern of worsening developmental outcomes as acculturation into

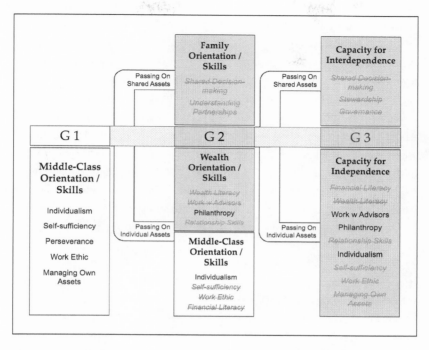

Figure 9-2: Adaptations of the family across generations, missing important skills for handling wealth.

American culture proceeds."[86] Although there are many complexities and some exceptions to the immigrant paradox, it appears to be a relatively common occurrence. The pattern finds increasing levels of substance abuse, association with other alienated youth, sexual acting-out, disregard for traditional family values, disrespect for elders, and waning interest in academic achievement as succeeding generations blend into American culture. Compared to next-generation youth who remain strongly attached to the family's traditional origins, more highly assimilated offspring show less favorable adjustment and, often, poorer outcomes including physical and mental health problems.

Americans usually assume the opposite is true. We push to assimilate immigrant children as fast as possible into English language and American life to "remediate" these presumed disadvantages. The real evidence is that young people grounded in the traditional values, cohesive family life, strong work ethic, and motivation for achievement present in their immigrant forebears apply themselves better, work harder, and navigate adolescence with greater resilience. G2 and G3 youth become more vulnerable to the lassitude American life can bring, unless they are taught new skills to handle their new environment.

The subtitle of a recent book on the immigrant paradox asks: "Is becoming American a developmental risk?"[87] The same question could easily be asked about wealth. Some older G2 children of the newly wealthy arrive with a firmer grounding in the work ethic, adversity, and knowledge of life's limitations than the Native siblings or generations yet to come. Like their ethnic counterparts, these bridge G2s harbor within them the strengths and immunities of their heritage culture. With any luck, many in G2 will preserve these strengths even as they adapt to an easier life.

By the time G3 arrives on the scene and grows into adolescence, however, those carryover strengths from the family's middle-class roots may be a vanishing memory. Loss of strong family values, lack of family communication, and failure to prepare heirs for wealth dissipates whatever strengths remain from the Immigrant life a few generations back.

Where to Get the Skills of Interdependence

It should now be clear why the acculturation strategy chosen by wealth's Pioneers is so fundamental to whether the complex set of family adaptations ever gets underway. Only those Immigrants opting for Integration have the insight for teaching both independence (from their heritage middle-class background) and interdependence (from their adoptive culture of wealth). Those who choose Avoidance rarely prepare their offspring for the independence truly needed to handle wealth. Plus, there is no preparation whatsoever for interdependence. Those G1s who choose Assimilation lose the grounding needed for both well-balanced independence and skillful interdependence.

COLLABORATION, COMMUNICATION, AND SHARED DECISION-MAKING

How then does a family from middle-class roots ever develop the skills to manage a complex set of shared assets? The task of the family is to foster the capacities needed to handle the interdependence of generational wealth. These include encouragement of family communication about wealth, a family orientation to shared decision-making and collaboration, shared knowledge about wealth's financial and legal management, and the many other activities that are a daily part of life with significant wealth.

We shall explore the details of shared decision-making and family governance in Chapter 10, including how these can be developed. The main point is that the groundwork for the family's future collaboration must be laid in the transitions between G1 and G2, and then from G2 to G3. All those individual-oriented skills necessary for independence must be matched with family-oriented skills and perspectives to teach interdependence.

The Lessons to Be Learned

Beginning with working- or middle-class Immigrants in G1, families of wealth need to undergo well-defined adaptations. By the time the third generation is ready to handle adult responsibilities, the family must reinforce twin capacities for *independence* and for *interdependence* as much as possible.

A strong capacity for self-determination and independence is the heritage G3 can receive from G1's roots in more modest economic circumstances. In addition, G3 must develop new capacities for sharing assets, making decisions together, managing partnerships, and collaborating for the benefit of the extended family. They then understand how the collective family can leverage its strengths, its teamwork, and its many components to foster the lives of individual family members.

As we shall discover in the next chapter, families who follow this roadmap grow beyond their roots in working- or middle-class life to work efficiently and effectively as a family of wealth. For them, the "shackles" of shared assets and collaborative decision-making are strong bonds that provide security and continuity across time and circumstance. These Integrators emphasize a unique combination of collective family activities, while also supporting each individual family member in finding his or her individual passion, purpose, and relationships in life.

They seek to create strong independence *in* family members and balanced interdependence *of* the family through skillful governance *by* the family. It is a maturation of the once-fragile outpost into a stable community that cares—in the deepest sense of the word—for its citizens. It is the next transformation for the family in its life with wealth.

CHAPTER 10

Fulfilling the Promise of Paradise

Bourdieau, the seminal French writer about culture, first articulated that people possess many forms of capital as part of their cultural identity and behavior.[88] Most affluent families think of their only "capital" as their wealth. They rarely contemplate the many other forms of capital that get transformed in the journey to paradise. Only a few fortunate families realize the importance of nurturing all of the family's tangible and intangible resources to avoid the shirtsleeves-to-shirtsleeves threat.

The components of this integrated approach cover the Financial, Intellectual, Social, and Human capitals of the family, shown in Figure 10-1.[89]

These four capitals of the family are easily remembered by the acronym F-I-S-H, suggested by the prominent wealth psychologist Lee Hausner.[90]

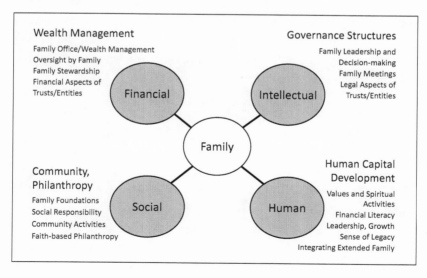

Wealth Management
Family Office/Wealth Management
Oversight by Family
Family Stewardship
Financial Aspects of
Trusts/Entities

Financial

Governance Structures
Family Leadership and
Decision-making
Family Meetings
Legal Aspects of
Trusts/Entities

Intellectual

Family

Community,
Philanthropy
Family Foundations
Social Responsibility
Community Activities
Faith-based Philanthropy

Social

Human Capital
Development
Values and Spiritual
Activities
Financial Literacy
Leadership, Growth
Sense of Legacy
Integrating Extended Family

Human

Figure 10-1: Nurturing the four capitals of the family.

Financial Capital

Financial capital is what most affluent families concentrate on. Yet it is really only one of four significant areas that must sustain the family and be well-managed in an integrated fashion. Assets accumulated over time require skillful management through the family's leadership in conjunction with financial advisors. Professional expertise may be provided by an accounting firm, financial planning firm, private bank, brokerage firm, single or multi-family office, registered independent advisory (RIA) firm, or a variety of other entities.

Part of the family's education is teaching the family the available options for wealth managers, the particular strengths and weaknesses of each, and the menu of offerings each provides. Families who grasp the benefits of truly integrated wealth management are generally able to optimize economies of scale and utilize best practices for the family's well-being. It takes real leadership for this to be accomplished within the first generation of the family's rise out of middle-class life. All too often during G1, management of the family's burgeoning financial capital is gradually cobbled together, piece-by-piece, by the wealth creator or his band of financial advisors. This typically creates a convoluted machine that ticks along with some degree of efficiency but has idiosyncrasies only the wealth creator knows how to manage. A crisis in many families occurs when this wealth contraption either breaks down (as many did during the bear market of 2007–2009) or its constructor becomes ill or dies without leaving instructions on its care or repair.

OVERSIGHT BY THE FAMILY

Optimal management of a family's financial capital also requires something else. Its professional management must include close, active involvement by the family's leadership. The family must know how its wealth is managed and must continue to provide effective oversight, including responsible decision-making for issues that cannot or should not be delegated to professional managers. At least some members of the family must have the knowledge needed to interface with its trusted advisors. This means the family must foster development of such leaders and empower them appropriately across generations.

RESPONSIBLE STEWARDSHIP BY THE FAMILY

Perhaps the most important factor in managing the family's financial capital is the one that typically gets the least nurturance. This element can easily override the activities of the family's wealth managers, no matter how skillful or efficient those managers may be. This factor is the degree to which the family acts as good stewards of its own wealth. Successful families sustaining their hard-earned outposts in paradise do so by acting prudently with their money, collectively as a family and individually in their personal lives. By making prudent financial decisions, including wise spending choices, the family helps preserve its financial capital and its sense of responsibility for its own financial well-being.

Good financial stewardship must occur in each generation. If this is not done, the wealth will eventually dissipate and the engine that sustains the family will sputter to a halt. As Dennis Jaffe outlines in his excellent book, *Stewardship in Your Family Enterprise,*[91] successful families foster responsibility for nurturing the family's wealth. They do this through teaching financial literacy and responsibility to each upcoming generation and each member entering the family from the outside through marriage or affiliation. The development of these activities is also part of fostering the human capital of the family (discussed below). Careful personal financial management embodies important values of the family such as self-responsibility, family cohesion, self-restraint, and work ethic.

FINANCIAL ASPECTS OF TRUSTS AND OTHER ENTITIES

Finally, as mentioned in Chapter 9, the family's complex planning for tax, estate, and business matters typically spawns legal entities to harbor the wealth. These trusts, partnerships, and other legal entities inevitably contain provisions that dictate how some part of the wealth is to be managed financially. Thoughtful integration of the family's financial capital, therefore, must be coordinated with the various entities the family creates. Effective wealth management must take these forces into account so that, for example, changes in tax laws impacting a family's income will be handled flexibly.

THE ROLES OF ACCULTURATION AND ADAPTATION

In managing just the financial capital of the family, the adjustment of the family's founders to the Land of Wealth must be accomplished successfully to at least some degree. A high level of individual and collective skill in financial management can only be possible for those who stay balanced in their view of wealth and its complexities.

———

Joan Lloyd had managed to cobble together a reasonable recovery with her wealth and her life over many years. With the help of a therapist knowledgeable about money and finance issues, she had gradually become more open and comfortable with her success and her modest wealth. She also built a good relationship with Rachel, who had married and had children of her own.

Joan's relationship with her sons remained rocky after the divorce from Ted. The secrets leaked out about the family's wealth, with her sons winding up blaming her more than Ted. Things got worse when Ted died of a heart attack at age seventy, triggering Ted's overly controlling estate planning which, as predicted, damaged the family dynamics. Ted Jr. was a punitive, difficult trustee who used his broad discretionary powers to tightly control Joan's distributions and those of the rest of the family. Joan resigned herself to coping with it as best she could. Her greatest goal was to help Rachel and her grandchildren be able to talk about whatever was important, including money, and to show generosity in whatever she did.

———

GOOD MANAGEMENT OF FINANCIAL CAPITAL REQUIRES FAMILIES to grasp the necessity of communicating openly about wealth, inculcating healthy skills for managing money, and making thoughtful decisions about wealth management. Many of these skills cannot be extrapolated easily from middle-class knowledge or viewpoints.

Already, in only this first capital of the family—the Financial Capital—the extended family must work to maintain that balance between independence of the individual and interdependence of the family.

Intellectual Capital

The family's intellectual capital may be considered the collective policies, structures, governance, and decision-making activities of the family. These rely on the intelligence and wisdom of its members and its advisers to manage the enterprise effectively. Successful multigenerational families of wealth put their heads together and leverage their intelligence to create governance systems for the family. Families do this for the same reason that cities or businesses must—because they share assets that support the family *community*. Significant wealth is not just more money; it is more complex money. With wealth comes the necessity for decision-making about the family's common assets and interests.

FAMILY LEADERSHIP AND DECISION-MAKING

During the initial migration and acculturation to wealth, the intellectual capital of the wealth creator determines what happens, perhaps in partnership with a capable spouse. Decisions about spending, investing, sharing, moving, withholding, distributing, protecting, risking, gifting, and managing the wealth constantly arise. Options must be weighed, based on circumstance, intelligence, commonsense, or whim. These decisions are *person-based,* that is, by a person (the wealth-creator) about other people (children, for example, or grandchildren). Those decisions may be benevolent or arbitrary, punitive or gracious, consistent with past decisions or changeable with the seasons or whoever within the family curries favor. The family has governance: It is vested in one leader who is typically strong-minded by nature and feels entitled to lead by virtue of having made the money.

However, person-based decision-making cannot sustain a family over generations. Too many inconsistencies creep in over time, whether from honest forgetting or spiteful favoritism. To survive, a family must function with a basic system of justice in place.

By G3, the family may have multiplied, along with its assets and its need for decision-making. Successful families make the fundamental shift to governance that is *policy-based*, no longer person-based. As with governments or with businesses, that means creating policies that are fair, wise, and consistent, independent of the person who happens to be sitting in the leader's chair at that moment.

EFFECTIVE STRUCTURES AND DOCUMENTS

Successful families learn to implement systems for this vision of fairness, stability, and wise management. They create family constitutions and mission statements to codify the family's values and establish the ground rules by which they will govern. They form family councils to oversee matters essential to the family's functioning. The council grapples with thorny issues and competing interests, deals with external threats, sets policies for long-term fairness, and makes decisions to be implemented. Like cities or businesses, these families govern themselves so the people under their care can go about their lives with security, comfort, and support.

LEADERSHIP DEVELOPMENT

Intellectual capital must, like financial capital, be groomed for the future. Far-thinking multigenerational families know that leadership must be renewed in every generation. They provide opportunities for developing up-and-coming family leaders, with policies for choosing and placing next-generation members in leadership positions. They support leadership development opportunities, just as any business must create a deep bench of executive management. And, like any business, this reserve of talent helps the family survive crises, such as the unexpected loss of an established leader. In doing so, the family prepares for one of the most crucial tasks of any enterprise: succession.

FAMILY MEETINGS AND ASSEMBLIES

Common activities that deploy the family's intellectual capital include regular meetings of the family itself, either as a collective gathering or, at the very least, of the leadership. This is a level of family communication beyond the more casual family meetings discussed in earlier chapters. Large multigenerational families hold family assemblies to provide education, hear about pressing matters, make and announce decisions, and retell the story of the family legacy. They host enjoyable events that cement family relationships and welcome newcomers, whether children or in-laws. These meetings allow conflicts to be aired and negotiated effectively so problems don't fester to poison family relationships.

LEGAL ASPECTS OF TRUSTS AND ENTITIES

Finally, the family's intellectual capital is nurtured by attention to an often-forgotten area of its own management. That is the policies and decision-making rules embedded in the formalized structures of the family's estate, legal, financial, and business documents. Wealthy families already are bound by a multitude of provisions that set certain policies, before the first keystroke is made for any mission statement or constitution. Families of wealth must be careful to create trusts, buy-sell agreements, prenuptial agreements, partnership agreements, and a host of other legal documents in ways that integrate wisely instead of in ways that conflict with each other. Just as trusts and entities include financial provisions that must be integrated with the family's wealth management, they also include legal and fiduciary provisions that must be integrated with the family's governance.

Social Capital

The family's social capital relates to the family's place in its community and in society. This is where the family's philanthropy resides along with the meaning of its wealth for society. For many families, this is one of the most important capitals. It provides a larger purpose for using wealth for the family's future, the family enterprise, and society.

Many of wealth's Immigrants and their offspring devote little time or attention in a proactive, purposeful way to philanthropy. Most charitable giving is driven by tax and estate planning rather than by values or purpose. Only a small proportion of wealth creators and their families have in-depth discussions about the meaning of the money, or how the family will contribute to the world. Moreover, many wealth managers shy away from these discussions as "not our business." More enlightened or skillful advisors understand this can be one of the most worthwhile parts of integrated wealth management.

MANY LEVELS OF INVOLVEMENT

Fostering the family's social capital involves activities from the micro to the macro level. At its most basic level, it involves the family elders teaching their children the types of money messages that create humility and a value-driven life for each person in the family. These messages help combat any entitlement and self-centeredness that may contaminate the next generation.

Going up a level, activities fostering social capital include parents and children volunteering their time and talents in the local community to help others less fortunate. It involves teaching children how to devote a portion of their allowance to charity, not just to themselves. Later, this may be matched by financial contributions to local charities or involvement in community action. There may be trips to disadvantaged or multicultural areas, whether in a different part of town or a different part of the globe. Seeing conditions of economic scarcity helps build humility in an environment of abundance. It also plants the seeds of charitable intent in the hearts of wealth's Immigrants and Natives alike.

At the family system level, activities organized around philanthropy may represent the broadest efforts of the family in their adaptation to wealth. Those families who devote time and energy to developing social capital commonly have a variety of planned giving methods and strategies. These include charitable giving at the level of individual family members or branches, the creation or funding of donor-advised funds, and the pooling of resources at the generational level in personal or family foundations.

FOUNDATIONS

Many HNW and UHNW families think of establishing a foundation as part of estate planning after the first- or second-to-die of the wealth-creating generation. They may do so for a variety of reasons: tax savings, diverting inheritance away from unprepared heirs, charitable intent, or (all too often) an effort to impose harmony upon the next generation. Well-meaning advisors will suggest the creation of foundations "as a way to keep the family together after you're gone," which is a message espoused by many family wealth experts and philanthropic organizations. For strong-willed wealth creators worried about the breakup of the family after parents are gone and wealth is distributed, this seems like a great way to exert control, even in death.

Unfortunately, this does not always work out. Without any advance preparation in shared decision-making or, worse yet, a long history of family discord, G2 and G3 siblings tend to act out their old rivalries around the foundation boardroom table. Creating the structure for collaboration, but not the skills, is only half the formula for success.

Families knowledgeable about balancing independence and interdependence do much better. They create family foundations that naturally pursue philanthropy as part of wealth. The foundation can oversee all of the family's philanthropic contributions, or individual members may do their own giving alongside the family foundation. These UHNW families make philanthropy a priority. They train each generation to participate in the activities and management of their family foundation. Their commitment becomes part of their family legacy. For some family members, philanthropic endeavors serve as their main purposeful activity in life, whether paid or unpaid. The most sophisticated family foundations have clear mission statements, values-driven philanthropy, formalized job responsibilities, and board functions.

PURPOSE FOR THE PIONEERS

Creation and management of family philanthropy can also serve as the next purpose in life for the wealth creators themselves, those Pioneers who already accomplished one amazing journey. A well-known modern example is the transition of Bill Gates from a founder of Microsoft to a founder of the Bill and Melinda Gates Foundation, along with his wife. His transition follows in the footsteps of famous industrialists-turned-philanthropists such as Andrew Carnegie. Many extremely successful businessmen and women see philanthropy as the next activity of entrepreneurship, not just as charitable giving.

SOCIALLY RESPONSIBLE AND/OR IMPACT INVESTING

Some families utilize their social capital to do more than charitable giving. They weave their sense of social responsibility into their life activities and their wealth management itself. They do this by focusing on socially aware actions and investments. They may actively engage in political or social causes, support community-action activities, invest in public-private partnerships, or fund educational ventures. These build opportunities for others to make economic journeys to better lands themselves. These generous families carefully consider the impact of their investments as a part of their overall investing strategy, motivated by a drive to elevate others less fortunate.

Socially responsible investing's roots extend back to the Religious Society of Friends (Quakers) who prohibited investing in the slave trade, as well as the prominent Methodist John Wesley who advocated against harming one's community through toxic or dangerous business practices. Starting from initiatives in the 1980s by such innovators as Amy Domini of Domini Social Investments and Joan Bavaria of Trillium Investment Management, hundreds of socially responsible investing opportunities, funds, and initiatives have been created to blend together a family's wealth *and* its place in society. These families enjoy having a way to integrate their values and their investment philosophy, creating a seamless interplay of what supports the family and what supports society.

FAITH-BASED PHILANTHROPY

The original and still-prominent method of fostering a family's social capital relies on the family's spiritual faith to light the way with wealth. Faith-based philanthropy draws together all the facets of a family's religious beliefs and practices in service of helping others in the world. A family's charitable giving and activities may be devoted to supporting social causes, faith initiatives (missionary work, ministries, support of churches or other religious organizations, and so on) or assistance to religious academic institutions, among other objectives. There are also networks of faith-based or faith-oriented giving, as in the Jewish Funders Network or the National Christian Foundation. Some families are simply active in supporting their local church, mosque, or temple, both financially and personally. These activities go behind integrating values with philanthropy to truly integrating faith and wealth.

Human Capital

Nurturing the family's human capital relates to what might be considered their "Department of Health, Education, and Welfare." In many ways, this may be the most important capital to foster, as it creates the foundation for sustaining wealth and families across generations. These activities bolster the family's ongoing efforts to build the dual capacities of independence and interdependence, preparing the next generation for living with wealth within the broader society of diverse economic groups.

FOSTERING THE VALUES AND SPIRITUAL CORE OF THE FAMILY

For many successful multigenerational families of wealth, the family's core values are grounded in formal or informal spiritual values. Whether in clearly religious activities or simply a strong emphasis on values, the family maintains a center that:

- Provides a cohesive set of values and ethics to encourage proper behavior, countering entitlement and self-centeredness.

- Encourages a sense of humility and humanity, countering wealth's tendency to make one feel special and unique.

- Provides a sense of community and belonging within society, off-setting the tendency to feel disconnected or superior.

- Provides a higher purpose and sense of perspective across time, off-setting wealth's focus on the material, the present, and the purely pleasurable.

Families of strong faith often feel that they are stewards of God's wealth, rather than true wealth owners themselves. This allows them to think and act humbly, with a long-term view about investments and philanthropic activities.

This is not to imply that all successful multigenerational families are strongly religious, which is not the case. It is simply to note that families who attend to members' spiritual core—in terms of cohesion, values clarification, sense of purpose, identity, and self-esteem—are less susceptible to what wealth counselor Thayer Willis aptly calls "the dark side of wealth."[92] When values-based messages about money, wealth, social responsibility, and life purpose are woven into the family enterprise, they lay a solid groundwork for education about financial skills and responsibilities.

FINANCIAL EDUCATION

Everyone at any economic level, including strangers in economic paradise, needs to be taught financial literacy in order to make informed decisions and manage their lives well. Successful multigenerational families of wealth simply take this very seriously for the extended community within their responsibility. They devote time and resources to providing education for family members to teach the basics of budgeting and personal financial management, along with other beneficial skills. Failure to teach these important skills fulfills the stereotype of the clueless "trust fund baby" who overspends, remains passive in his or her own wealth management, and refuses to work productively in conjunction with advisors.

Some families design and implement their own methods for teaching these skills, sometimes in collaboration with wealth advisors who provide guidance and resources. There are also sophisticated programs for financial literacy training that families can access.[93] Standalone one-time educational events and financial "boot camps" for teenagers or young adults (offered by prominent wealth management firms) provide some help to families who haven't done much to educate their up-and-coming family members. More sophisticated programs at prominent universities such as Wharton or Stanford offer intensive programs in understanding investments, family business, and high-end wealth management. The best family educational programs provide age-appropriate training, beginning prior to age fourteen, and continue with increasing sophistication through early adulthood.

———

Barb Spinelli loved spending time with her two grandchildren, ages ten and eight. One of their favorite activities together was what she called "The Treasure Hunt."[94] They would go to a shopping mall in the morning and, on the way over, plan strategies. She would help them establish a budget based on how much she was willing to spend on them, plus allowance money they'd saved. They then would discuss what they wanted to buy. At the mall, they would comparison shop, evaluating whether they really wanted this toy or that piece of clothing, but not buying yet. Barb would instruct them to write down how much the final price of an item would be, with tax, so they had to calculate the real cost.

Over lunch, Barb would discuss with the kids what each child might purchase. Each had to explain what they would choose and why, making sure the total was within the budget. Even if Barb didn't fully agree with their logic, as long as they could state their views and their choice was reasonably appropriate for their age, she would let them make their purchases after lunch. Occasionally she encouraged them to pool their money to buy something together, which meant they had to learn to share and collaborate.

Sometimes the toy would break before they even made it home. Sometimes the glittery shirt would be worn maybe once. However, it was more important to Barb that her grandchildren learned to calculate, to evaluate things critically, to restrain the impulse to buy on the spot, to learn from mistakes, and to take responsibility for decision-making. What her grandchildren loved more than her money was having her full attention and her trust. Everybody always won the Treasure Hunt.

PROMOTING LEADERSHIP AND GROWTH

As mentioned under Intellectual Capital, the elders within families play an important role in developing its future leaders and generally fostering the growth of young people within the family. Even if the next generation doesn't intend to become an essential role in the family's leadership, the family should still provide educational opportunities, career counseling, and business contacts designed to help young people find their place in life and manage their individual wealth. Since finding purpose is a central value for such families, activities that allow younger members to make accurate, focused, and timely choices regarding their careers will be helpful. Such avenues include recommendations about where to go for academic testing or placement, referrals for special services, or even career or aptitude assessment. Within the family, there may be opportunities to participate on committees or task forces to help the family council on special projects or for upcoming family meetings.

INTEGRATION OF NEW FAMILY MEMBERS

Just as with any community, people are constantly entering and exiting the family over time. Entrances occur from two general directions. One is from children born into the family, the creation of new lives who are truly Native to the Land of Wealth. The second portal is for people brought into the family via marriage or other close affiliation, such as adoption or civil unions.

Most families normally think about how they will integrate their children—bloodline citizens of the family—into the family and the family enterprise. Successful multigenerational families do this through gradually expanding:

- Financial education.
- Participation in family meetings and assemblies.
- Responsibility for holding seats on the family foundation.
- Interaction with the family's advisors and trustees.
- Educational trips that teach the legacy and values of the family.

Families may have rules or expectations, for example, that children over the age of fourteen can be part of family meetings with the proper preparation about codes of conduct and privacy of information. Or, that joining the Family Council is possible over the age of twenty-one.

Families who genuinely foster their human capital also offer most if not all of these activities to its Transplant in-laws as well. Most in-laws marry in from the middle class, requiring orientation and education to adapt. But some may be already citizens of the Land of Wealth as Natives born to other wealthy families. Being Native is no guarantee they've been trained well in those key skills of wealth literacy, open communication, or initiative. They may need as much orientation as any Immigrant to paradise.

THE ISSUE OF IN-LAWS

In-laws and stepchildren must contend with the cultural mistrust by the wealthy toward those who marry in. Despite originally being Immigrants themselves, wealthy families quickly become wary of outsiders. Once in the Land of Wealth, the family naturally starts to guard itself against those who want to partake of their bounty without being a productive and loyal member of the clan. This is completely understandable. Any bountiful land will naturally attract the unsavory and the unscrupulous.

There are, however, two problems with this defensive perimeter. The noted family wealth advisor, Jay Hughes, reminds families that it was Immigrant dreams and Immigrant sweat that led the family to wealth.

Those who come to the family as Immigrants, not Natives, may ironically be the best hope for the family's renewed success over time. Fresh thinking, work ethic, and new energy may be more likely to come from those who marry into the family than from those who arise from the family itself.[95]

Second, mistrust by the family creates the very conditions known to impede successful adaptation of individuals to a new environment. Remember that one of the strongest determinants of how well immigrants are able to adapt to a receiving culture is the degree to which the new culture is welcoming or rejecting. Harsh prenuptial agreements, cold shoulders at wedding parties, legal barricades by advisors, and the resulting defensiveness on the part of new in-laws are wealth's equivalent of immigration laws, border protection, and the resentment they engender. The well-known stresses of marrying into a wealthy family make perfect sense from a cultural perspective.

Families that do know how to foster their Human Capital develop methods for introducing in-laws and stepchildren to the extended family system, usually in a progressive manner that manages the risks of having a newcomer join a closely-knit system. These families often use their closest wealth advisors to educate in-laws, starting with limited information and then allowing greater knowledge of the family's enterprise over time. At family assemblies, in-laws and their children are welcomed, invited to experience the family's leadership system in action, encouraged to participate in shared activities, and are introduced to the history and ways of the family.

All of these methods of acculturation serve to help the Transplant adjust to wealth and to the family system in a gradual, measured way.

Gina's husband William and his family welcomed her into the large family assembly held each year around Thanksgiving. These events reminded her of a much bigger, noisier version of her own family's casual family meetings each summer. She loved watching the five-member Family Council, drawn from different generations, present information to the assembly and listen to the collective concerns, questions, and suggestions. She even spoke up nervously a few times, when she had a point to make.

After two years, Gina volunteered to participate on an investment-committee task force, where she put her business acumen to good use. She eventually was asked to be an ad hoc member of the Family Council where, after a vacancy opened up for a member of her generation, she was nominated to become a full member. Even though she was not a bloodline member of her husband's family, she was accepted and respected.

SUCCESSFUL UHNW FAMILIES KNOW THE KEY TO SUSTAINING WEALTH is not just about when or how to inform in-laws (or potential in-laws) about money. It's about helping these Transplants absorb the history, values, attitudes, relationships and behaviors of the family. In other words, it's about helping newcomers acculturate to the Land of Wealth they now live in. A welcoming family doesn't leave each new Immigrant to flounder in his or her adjustment to new circumstances. A welcoming family actively and intentionally supports the acculturation process.

FOSTERING THE FAMILY LEGACY

If all a family shares are its financial assets, entropy will eventually win out. Succeeding generations will increasingly go their own, separate way as they divide the wealth. Families need something more, something that evokes a desire for genuine connection, beyond interdependence.

The story of the family—its traditions and rituals, its values, its history of risk and reward, its times of crisis and resolution—must be told and retold to reinforce the ongoing legacy of the family. The legacy must also be actively lived in each generation, through maintaining principles based on the family's philanthropy, how it conducts its businesses, how it engages in its communities, how it cares for its family members, and how it raises good stewards of its wealth.

The story of the family's wealth creation and the principles that bind the family are more helpful than most families realize. The family's legacy is a narrative that supports a sense of cohesion, purpose, and values. The narrative creates a shared sense of community and contributes to the ongoing success of the family. These are the *real* bonds that pay dividends for the family.

The purpose is not to pump up egotism and feed an unhealthy spirit of "we are special." That happens all too easily—whether the family wants it or not—simply from the amount of wealth the family has accumulated. Retelling and refreshing the family narrative grounds the family in the values of those Immigrants to wealth who first established the outpost in paradise. Legacy provides a sense of continuity for multiple generations and, most importantly, engenders the appreciation and humility necessary to live competently with wealth.

Processes that foster the family legacy include creating and maintaining written, oral, or video histories of the family's wealth history and recording the ongoing accomplishments of the family enterprise. Efforts in this regard include videotaped interviews of the elders discussing the family legacy, coffee-table books documenting the family history in text and pictures, and periodic sharing of stories during family assemblies and family meetings. As each generation arises and new members join the family, they will feel inspired to add their individual stories of leadership, accomplishment, and spiritual endeavor. These teach the history of the family and, in doing so, the values of the family.

The Role of Community in Building Family Capital

Ethnic immigrants have one advantage over economic Immigrants. They are far more likely to receive help from a community of fellow immigrants who have made the journey before them. These communities offer the opportunity to be surrounded by people who speak their language yet can teach newcomers the cultural ropes. This familiarity often helps reduce their acculturation stress and facilitates adaptation to their new culture. That's what the Welcome Wagon used to be for, after all.

Economic Immigrants, however, may or may not receive much helpful advice upon moving to their new culture. The outside world thinks the wealthy have lots of community, but, in reality, there is little at a deep level. There are precious few opportunities to share perspectives on the journey, solicit support in making the adaptation, or learn from peers about best practices for the dilemmas of wealth. This creates a unique challenge for any family trying to build the many functions needed to foster the four capitals.

A favorable development in the past fifteen years may reflect how the Land of Wealth is becoming more multicultural, supportive, and community-focused. Since the 1990s, a growing number of organizations offer the chance to learn from peers and experts about family dynamics, philanthropy, family business, and family governance. Such organizations include the Institute for Private Investors, CCC Alliance, Family Wealth Alliance, Family Office Exchange, Campden Conferences, Family Office Association, and TIGER 21, to name just a few.

There are other organizations that provide peer support for successful professionals and members of family businesses, since these are the very people who are migrating to the Land of Wealth. They include the Young Presidents Organization, Women Presidents Organization, Family Business Network, and the many conferences and events where business-owning families can gather to exchange ideas and hear about best practices for fostering the next generation.

Next-generation members—essentially those who are Natives to wealth—are also finding new organizations for support. Resource Generation, 21/64, the Redwoods Initiative, the Threshold Foundation, and a variety of socially progressive or philanthropic groups have sprung up to provide community for heirs. There are also faith-oriented groups for wealth such as Harvest Time.

In addition to these peer-sponsored activities, many financial firms at the higher levels of wealth are offering client events where families can meet and learn from speakers. The best events also include the chance to talk to each other about personal topics such as G2 and G3 education, women and wealth, and family issues. Financial firms are often very nervous about whether clients will talk to each other or feel their privacy is being violated. Once in the room together, many clients quickly find they'd rather talk to each other about their family dilemmas than hear from advisors about these very personal issues. I have been involved in many of these events, and they usually generate great energy on the part of the attendees. As families listen to the setbacks and successes of others in paradise, they find relief that they are not alone.

All these burgeoning opportunities bring a warm sense of community to families trying to build a healthy system together.

Fulfilling the Promise of Paradise

If HNW and UHNW multigenerational families want to sustain and grow their wealth over succeeding generations, they must foster the four family capitals—Financial, Intellectual, Social, and Human—which requires ongoing focused effort, drawn from a collective spirit.

Emerging research is confirming that the many activities described in this chapter are the very components global family enterprises use to sustain themselves across generations.[96] When families are able to shift how they function to support *all* of their capital—financial and otherwise—they have adapted themselves to operate well in the Land of Wealth. They haven't abandoned the most valuable aspects of their middle-class roots. They have transformed themselves to function successfully in the very different culture of wealth.

CHAPTER 11

Strangers in Paradise No Longer

The proverb "shirtsleeves to shirtsleeves in three generations" is a sobering reminder about the difficulty of sustaining family wealth, in America and around the world. Yet our common assumption that wealth destroys families may not be accurate. The real culprit may be that families are unprepared to adapt to wealth. With much to learn and little guidance, they watch their wealth and their family bonds vanish.

———

Phil Spinelli, now in his late seventies, emerged from the security area at the Cleveland airport, on the way to his gate. He heard an old familiar voice call out his name. It was Joan Lloyd, on her way back from a trip to Rachel's family. They had lost touch many years ago, though he had heard indirectly that she and Ted had divorced. Phil and Joan spent the next hour catching up.

Joan described how she had rebuilt her life after the divorce. She described the damage to the family relationships, and she admitted how hard it had been to handle the windfall that had entered their lives. With much help, she had gradually come to accept and work with the money she had received. The fallout from Ted's death in terms of estate planning was a constant source of frustration in an otherwise peaceful old age.

Phil shared how things had gone better for himself and his family. He also described how Max had burned through much of his share of SteriMetrix's sale, winding up in a comfortable but not luxurious retirement village close to where he grew up. Max's wife had died, and neither of his sons visited him once the money was depleted. Only his daughter Alicia still came to see him, now that Max could no longer use his wealth to control, intimidate, or impress. Max's grandchildren were spending through whatever was left in their hands. Soon the Morgan Family would no longer be considered among the wealthy.

"We really didn't know what we were getting into, did we?" Phil said to Joan wryly.

"Well, Max and I thought we did." she said. "You were the one who felt like you didn't know what to do." Joan smiled. "You were the smart one."

———

VIEWED THROUGH THE NEW LENS OF CULTURAL ADAPTATION, THE drastic failure rate of generations of wealth's Immigrants and Natives becomes understandable. It's hard to succeed at tasks you don't know exist and which no one ever prepared you to tackle.

Understanding wealth as economic culture, not just as class, allows us to have a new roadmap through the Land of Wealth. Borrowing from the teachings of cross-cultural psychology, we can now see that the real challenges are to integrate the old and the new, first at the individual level and then at the family level. This natural sequence of generational adaptation requires a deliberate and conscious selection of the best from two sources: the family's heritage of economic hardship, and its new culture of security, stability, and opportunity. These insights have been hiding in plain sight all along, just waiting to help individuals, couples, and families face the many challenges of wealth.

The Opportunities Ahead

The community of advisors to families of wealth—attorneys, estate planners, wealth managers, philanthropic advisors, psychologists, and others—has always struggled to shift clients' middle-class perspective to a wealth perspective effectively. By using the cultural model of wealth, we may now have the opportunity to develop more persuasive explanations, better ways of engaging skeptical clients. My hope is that we find intuitive, innovative methods for explaining this new approach to life, wealth, and family, based on the metaphor of Immigrants and Natives first articulated by Dennis Jaffe and myself.

If we can accomplish this as an industry, those arriving in the Land of Wealth would receive better guidance in many areas: how to adjust more smoothly, how to incorporate affluence into their parenting skills, how to nurture the budding Natives under their roof, and how to adapt the family for success across generations. The opportunities for peer communities and social support may also improve as people grasp the critical nature of these benefits for helping families adapt. Not only would this mean that wealth would not be seen as so inevitably toxic, it would allow each generation to be more productive managing the fortune under its stewardship. This would greatly benefit society as much as the individual and the family.

The Evolving Land of Wealth

There is another reason for optimism, based on the increasingly multicultural nature of the Land of Wealth. The past decade has been hard on migration to wealth. Fewer people have been able to make the journey successfully, and the distance to be navigated is larger than ever. Yet, the formerly monolithic white male culture of wealth is diversifying.

The burgeoning influx of women to wealth, in particular, has important implications for families and their adaptation. Entering in record numbers, women will exert an ever-stronger influence on the culture of wealth itself. Naturally attuned to the core values conducive to helping families succeed, women are more likely to emphasize the value of family relationships, effective parenting, open communication, and the importance of financial education from an early age. Their prioritizing of parenting and familial relationships can greatly accelerate the adoption of the cultural model for understanding wealth's challenges, especially in the oft-neglected area of family *interdependence*. Fostering *independence* has long been a male priority. It's time that family interconnectedness, decision-making, and collaboration were more strongly emphasized for wealth.

The Way Forward

The cultural model of wealth adds substantially to the growing body of knowledge about wealth in families. It points the way for families attempting to secure their place in the Land of Wealth. This new roadmap greatly enhances their chances of success, revealing what they need to do more clearly through effective adaptation. The way forward is clearer. In the process, more families can reach and remain in economic paradise, no longer feeling like strangers in a foreign land.

They are home.

A Short History of the 80/20 Pattern of Wealth in the United States

THE ROOTS OF THE 80/20 PATTERN OF WEALTH IN THE UNITED STATES date back to the early 1800s when, as an emerging economy, wealth in America arose largely due to entrepreneurship and agricultural development. With inheritance laws favoring the breakup of large estates—unlike the European tradition—Alexis de Tocqueville reported in his book *Democracy in America* that "the rich daily rise out of the crowd and constantly return hither."[97]

By the late 1800s, the 80/20 proportion of new to old wealth was becoming well established.[98] The tremendous rise in industrialization led to the creation of Gilded Age fortunes. Names we now associate with Old Money began as very New Money: Andrew Carnegie, John Jacob Astor, Cornelius Vanderbilt, John D. Rockefeller, J.P. Morgan. These captains of industry were their era's equivalent of Bill Gates of Microsoft, Warren Buffett of Berkshire Hathaway, Sergey Brin of Google, and Jeff Bezos of Amazon, arising from middle economic classes to extreme wealth in the span of a few decades.

The preponderance of New Money over Old Money continued through the first part of the Twentieth Century. The march of industrialization was matched by fortunes generated by oil-and-gas discovery and financial investment performance, continuing through the Roaring Twenties. So many middle-class people started to achieve wealth on paper that the ranks of the affluent swelled with new versus inherited wealth, even as the heirs of Gilded Age industrialists were proliferating. Then the Great Depression served as The Great Leveler, sending many of the top 10 percent of wealth-holders back down the economic scale. In subsequent decades, the ranks of Old Money among America's wealthy swelled as inheritance factors reasserted themselves.

World War II and the prosperity that followed revived the upward migration to wealth. The tremendous surge in wealth creation from the early 1980s to the present has, along with moderation in the estate tax laws, kept the percentage of wealth acquirers around the longstanding baseline of approximately 80 percent

Recommendations for Thriving as a Family

STRANGERS IN PARADISE EXPLAINS WHY AND HOW FAMILIES OF WEALTH must undergo significant cultural adaptation, akin to that of ethnic immigrants migrating to a new homeland. The book is largely focused on outlining the model for understanding the process, rather than a detailed how-to guide for coping with wealth.

The following recommendations are directed to readers who are individuals, couples, or families wanting a few specifics on how to accomplish the adaptation. These address what *you* can do to help you and your children adapt to wealth.

ONE: BE CONSCIOUS OF YOUR OWN ADJUSTMENT PROCESS

Before you, as the Immigrant to wealth, can begin to assist your children, focus upon your own adjustment to your new circumstances. Keep a clear-eyed perspective on the cultural transitions you are undergoing. You may have to discard some no-longer-appropriate attitudes of your upbringing, creating space to integrate the best aspects of where you came from and where you now find yourself.

For example, it may serve you well to maintain the healthy aspects of the work ethic you learned from your own parents or background. Be wary of fully embracing retirement and a life of leisure, however much you may feel you deserve it. Find new purpose to keep you busy. It will bring pleasure to your workday, and it will keep you stimulated and challenged. Your children need to see you maintaining purpose despite the financial resources at your disposal. Be an example that money is not the only motivation to work hard to achieve goals. You can still enjoy leisure activities and family time, but demonstrate that balancing purpose, family, and recreation is the best use of abundance.

You may need to learn to make new choices about spending and saving in light of your new affluence. Enjoy being released from the limitations of your background, but remain thoughtful about your spending decisions and the messages you send to your children with each large purchase. Make sure you can explain the decision-making behind your choices and that the process is not driven solely by emotion or whim. Resist the temptation to use money to allay all pain, stress, or problem-solving for yourself or your children. Think: What would a middle-class person do to show caring or support, if he or she didn't have money? At crucial times your presence may be more important than your wealth.

To model strong values to your children and grandchildren, develop a healthy perspective on self-responsibility and philanthropy. Spend time understanding your values, what drove you before you had wealth, and what may need to shift in propelling the next phase of your life *with* wealth. Make sure old habits and motivations still serve you rather than hold you back.

Surrender any residual hostile envy related to being wealthy that may be left over from your background. Move beyond unhealthy or stereotyped attitudes about economic groups (yours or anyone else's) to an appreciation of people separate from issues of power or class. Find strong, secure role models who exemplify the best aspects of wealth and life. If you do wish to devote energy or resources to economic class issues among groups or individuals, be able to articulate your goals and values to your children. Make this a part of the story of your journey and your legacy.

Work toward a balanced appreciation of wealth, understanding its limitations and its many complexities. Be open to learning about best practices and new attitudes related to wealth in today's world.

TWO: TEACH THE NEXT GENERATION

Understand and implement the preparation of the next generation in three main areas: development of good values, education of new skills, and the central role of family communication. If not already sure, learn how to inculcate values of self-responsibility, orientation to family, social responsibility, and delay of gratification, because the next generation growing up with affluence will absolutely need to learn these things from you. Provide money skills and financial education for your children from an early age, as well as modeling open and honest communication when talking about money and wealth. In doing so, underscore that abundant resources must be managed using skill and knowledgeable decision-making

This apprenticeship needs to occur long before your children reach adulthood. Money messages and values are internalized much earlier in life than you may think. Starting to talk about values when people are age eighteen or twenty-five risks being too late. When faced with an impulse to buy things you may not need, say in front of your children or grandchildren, "Let me put this aside and think about it for a day. Then I'll know whether I want it, or maybe I'll realize I don't need it." Talking out loud about your financial thought-process teaches decision-making about spending, saving, your values, and how you manage needs versus wants. Other healthy money messages include:

- Just because we have the money doesn't mean we can or should buy anything we want.

- It's not the price of things; it's the value of things.

- I don't think this represents a good value, so I'm not going to buy it.

- Let's check our budget and see if this is something we can fit in right now. (Even if you know you can easily afford it, it is a good thought process for children to hear and internalize.)

- Yes it's nice but I don't really need it. There are better things we can spend our money on.

Messages that build solid values include being able to talk comfortably about having "more than enough" when children are present. When you are happy about being able to afford something you normally couldn't afford in the past, it can be helpful to articulate this to the child who is listening, by saying:

- It feels really special for me to be able to buy this [expensive car, expensive house, vacation home, etc.] because my family was never be able to do this when I was growing up; or

- I've worked hard for this, and it would be enjoyable for us to be able to have this as part of our lives; or

- I feel very grateful that I've come to a point where I can afford this now; or
- I've looked at our budget and found we can afford to do this now without straining our finances.

Children of wealth see their parents buying something expensive, but they don't often hear the backstory on how or why the decision was made, or how this fits in with their parents' life experience and activities. These types of messages reinforce positive values by linking the purchase to hard work, gratitude, appreciation, and healthy self-esteem.

If trusts are to be part of your children's lives, begin discussion of this well before the event occurs, if possible. Discuss and model being focused, dependable, and responsible beneficiaries of trusts, advocating for engaged relationships with trustees and knowledge of the roles and responsibilities that are part of being an informed beneficiary. Instead of worrying helplessly about the demotivating influence of trusts, discuss frankly how trust income is to be managed like any other income source, as just one part of life. Describe the family's values, stressing that everyone works in paid or nonpaid activities, simply because it is the right thing to do. Teach the nuts and bolts of trusts, explain how trustees and beneficiaries can work together responsibly, and demystify the process so your children understand the context in which trusts are useful. Look for (the many) examples around you in life or literature about unhealthy uses of trusts. Use these for teachable moments with your children so they will know the difference.

Watch for messages you convey about money in relationships. Spend time teaching how wealth makes trusting people harder but not impossible. It is not helpful to provide warnings about others' intentions without also teaching them what to do about it in positive ways. Be careful to teach your children how to create opportunities for others to demonstrate their trustworthiness and devotion based on friendship or love, instead of need or greed. Show that a cherished friend is more valuable than money. Discuss what makes a good life partner and, if necessary, how to extract yourself from unhealthy relationships. The message in all these skills is that your children deserve to have loving, trusted relationships because they are worth it.

Provide some type of spiritual or religious foundation for personal values, appreciation of other people, and perspective on success and wealth. As part of this, provide early and ongoing opportunities to learn about and interact with people of varying economic levels with empathy, humility, and appreciation. Teach and model the use of the family's resources to benefit others in society, emphasizing the commonality of humanity rather than differences or stratifications.

THREE: HONOR THE NEXT GENERATION'S EXPERIENCES AND POINT OF VIEW

Understand that your children are growing up in a different economic culture than you did, subject to different rules. Be careful about judging their behavior or attitudes on the basis of circumstances present in your upbringing. Try to see some validity in their viewpoint. It may help level the playing field across generations.

Remember that your children or grandchildren may feel intimidated by those who created the wealth—perhaps by *you*. Resist elevating yourself too much as the one who made the money, owns the money, deserves the money, and accomplished what few in the family are ever likely to duplicate. Show them that you are proud of accomplishments they strive hard to achieve.

G2 and G3 have to find their rightful place at the table. Values, experience, and perspective cannot be inherited like eye color, or taken on faith just because parents or grandparents say so. Desirable values and perspectives must be adapted and made real in the present, not just spoken of with reverence for the past. You know your world from your perspective, colored by where you came from. They know the present and the future in ways you cannot. Allow them a voice in determining how the family can adapt to the present world, and later a role that honors their unique talents and contribution.

Realize that your children and grandchildren may need skills for sharing, decision-making, and collaboration, particularly if you plan for situations where they will share assets. If possible, from an early age, create opportunities for them to learn how to negotiate and collaborate with others to manage responsibilities. Restrain your temptation to take over or control these learning opportunities, especially when mistakes are made. Remember your own mistakes and how much you learned from those experiences. Sharing and collaborating are hard for most people—give it time, seek input from others if needed. Develop these skills in yourself and your offspring. Everyone will benefit no matter what happens with the wealth.

Recognize and accept that G2s and G3s live as a stereotyped minority as people with wealth. Offer strategies to help family members know how to deal with this. This also applies to in-law spouses who migrate into the family and need the same type of education, support, and assistance with cultural adaptation and safe haven. In doing so, create a communal family legacy that will sustain and inspire your family.

ADAPTING TO THE NEW WORLD

Consider these aspirations some of your guideposts on the road to healthy adaptation with wealth. Wealth need not be feared. It can be managed and embraced. The key lies in the family's learning to adapt, preserving the heritage of the Old Country of economic hardship, while adopting new strategies for wealth.

Understanding Family Meetings

If you are ready to consider meeting as a family to work on wealth, here are some of the steps involved:

In Discussing Wealth, "One and Done" Doesn't Work.

Family meetings need to be an ongoing process. Start with the idea of beginning a process rather than holding an event. It will get easier over time and the family will begin to look forward to it.

Choose a Comfortable Setting.

Don't feel intimidated that family meetings need to be a complicated, expensive or highly formal process like a series of business conferences. Many families get together on a casual basis for a meal at a restaurant or during shared vacations, during which they do the work of the family together. Meetings can be as informal or structured as you wish or as your circumstances require. The most important thing is to meet and communicate.

Establish Agreement for Privacy and Trust.

Many families hesitate to begin because they fear that whatever personal and financial information discussed will quickly escape into the friendships, extended family, or partner relationships that family members have outside the meeting. Without some agreement on maintaining the family's boundaries, private family communication is over before it begins. The first conversation, then, is to discuss and establish a privacy agreement, ensuring that the family's private conversations will remain private. A prefatory comment by a parent to each adult child might go something like this:

> I/We would like to begin conducting family meetings with you and your siblings about important issues in our family, including talking about money. We would like to do this because we feel it's time for us to discuss more openly the family's wealth, our estate planning, how we can all understand and have skills

for managing money, our values, and other matters that may come up over time as a family. We are excited to begin doing this, though we also are a bit nervous about it. We're not quite sure how to address everything. But we want to try.

In order to do this, we need to feel comfortable that what is discussed in our meetings will remain private within the family. We know you have [close friends/your girlfriend/your boy-friend/your wife/your husband/your wife's parents] with whom you share confidences and important information. We don't want to interfere in those relationships, but we do need to feel that our private business isn't going to be discussed with others in all its detail. We'd like to ask you to hold what we talk about in confidence, allowing us to maintain a high level of trust while working on the issues. Otherwise it's going to be hard to share information.

What are your thoughts about this? Would you be willing to agree to this?

Then listen and, if need be, negotiate the boundaries. If your children are able to promise complete privacy with no disclosure to anyone about the meetings, then you are set. If grown children admit that they cannot keep the fact of the meetings private from spouses but don't have to disclose what goes on, that may be good enough. Sometimes a compromise allowing disclosure of generalities is possible, with the spouse knowing that "my family is meeting to talk about some private matters includ-ing some things about money/estate planning/the family business, but I've agreed to hold the information private for now." If an adult child admits it would be impossible or unreasonable not to tell the person he or she is most intimate with, you then have to decide what to do.

Remember that adults have the right to decide the level of trust and communication they have in their closest relationships. If your adult child has a loving partner and they have decided to maintain open-ness as part of the relationship, you need to respect that and appreci-ate that your child values communication in relationships. Negotiate as best you can.

If accurate, you could begin by reassuring your child that his or her spouse will—in all likelihood—be invited into the meetings in the future. Including spouses may occur once the initial discussions have proven fruitful and/or their need to know means it is time to include them. You can tell your child that advisors often recommend beginning with the nuclear family, at least for a while.

Be frank about your own need to be assured about privacy in light of how hard the process of disclosure may be for you. Also keep in mind that your mistrust about family members' lying about maintaining privacy may be your issue more than theirs. It may require trust on your part to institute communication without having ironclad guarantees. Your children may be impressed with your willingness to try it their way, despite what they always have known is your skepticism about loyalty and trust. You also have the right to modulate the timing and degree of disclosure of detailed information, dependent upon how solid the family boundaries are for privacy and your willingness to tolerate uncertainty around this.

An unexpected payoff of the initial privacy discussion is that other family members' pride in being approached and included for these discussions may increase. To be trusted is to feel respected. People sometimes rise to the occasion when asked to hold confidences. They know they are being asked something precious, which they do not want to damage. The very act of approaching cherished family members to participate in crucial conversations may deepen family relationships before the first meeting even begins.

Use Clear Ground Rules for Communication.

Families differ widely in their habits and history of communication. Some families speak respectfully to each other yet are able to be open and direct. Some families enjoy the rough-and-tumble of teasing, profanity, speaking over each other, and yelling. But because they are equally active in their love of each other, no one feels hurt. Other families use spiteful, sarcastic, or cold communication that promotes conflict over caring. When conversations are not safe or respectful, people will legitimately refuse to participate.

At the end of this Appendix is a set of ground rules I've used in countless family meetings with clients over the years. The thread that runs through each rule is respect: respect for people and respect for the delicate process of family communication. Most family wealth

consultants use variations of these ground rules in facilitating family meetings. Use these, or create a similar set of rules for your family.

The ground rules should be discussed and agreed upon at the beginning of each family meeting, until it is clear the family knows and follows the rules. Do not proceed to any family agenda items until and
unless all participants agree to the rules. Otherwise, there is a risk of
negative events such as yelling matches, abusive language, or finger
pointing that shuts down communication. Ground rules are truly the
grounding of the meeting and of the family. Find your footing first, and
then start the journey together.

Note that all families will need to be reminded of the ground rules
periodically. Expect to enforce one or more of the rules at various times
throughout the first meeting and occasionally thereafter. Families without a strong history of healthy, productive communication must learn
to *use* the rules, not just know about them. Good leadership and proper
facilitation of family meetings requires diplomatic yet firm enforcement
of the rules for everyone. Failure to enforce ground rules will damage
the meeting and the credibility of the leadership. When the family sees
everybody is accountable for following the agreed-upon procedure,
meetings will feel safe and go smoothly.

If you feel unsure about your skills and need help to jump-start the
process, by all means seek it out. Assistance can range from hiring a
psychologically-minded attorney, accountant, or financial advisor to
having a wealth counselor or financial therapist assist for the first few
meetings. It's better to create success from the beginning than to risk
establishing a history of conflict, which may lead family members to
run from the process and never return. A list of financial therapists can
be found through the Financial Therapy Association (*www.financialthe-
rapyassociation.org*) or upon recommendation from your financial firm
or trusted advisor.

GROUND RULES FOR FAMILY MEETING COMMUNICATION

1. **Be present:** Demonstrate your respect and commitment by setting
   aside potential distractions. Turn off phones, cell-phones, laptops,
   and any other electronics. If you need to be reached in case of

emergency for your children or business, arrange an emergency contact person to intercept calls during the meeting. Be present at scheduled times of beginning and ending in meetings so the meeting can get the job done. Devote room in your life and your heart to this meeting.

2. **Be respectful in words, body language, and action:** Speak respectfully, pay attention when someone else is talking, and avoid jumping in to finish sentences. Avoid negative body language such as rolling your eyes, shaking your head, or conveying other emotional reactions. If it happens despite your effort to control such reactions, follow up by talking directly about the concern beneath your reaction. Keep profanity to a minimum. If you have a question or point to make, wait for an opening, or raise a hand to indicate you have something to bring up. You will appreciate it when others act the same way while *you* are talking.

3. **Be willing to edit what you say so it comes across better:** Saying anything and everything you feel under the guise of "honesty" can simply be a license to attack. Deliver your points with tact and respect. You will be more likely to be heard. Appropriate editing of your message will reduce the chances that other people will feel defensive, which can quickly lead to breakdowns in communication.

4. **Own your views as your own:** Make "I" statements rather than broad, global statements that imply only you know the truth, or that something is "obvious." Saying "everyone knows that is ridiculous" is unhelpful and destructive to communication. Saying, "I really disagree with what you just said" is more honest and may be more accurate. If others do share your views, it will be clear that there is a shared perspective on an issue. If others do not share your view, you may then open up to new viewpoints or solutions.

5. **Avoid indirect communication:** Families are notorious for allowing indirect communication and alliances. Indirect communication allows avoidance of conflict rather than resolution of problems. It can, in fact, make small problems grow into feuds between allied camps. Deal directly with whomever you are having the conflict, whenever possible.

6. Listen: Listening is a skill that must be practiced, because it pays off tremendously in effective communication. Be willing to demonstrate that you understand what the other person is saying before making your own point. You may find you are reacting to what you *believe* someone said, not what he or she really said. When someone else is saying something you disagree with, make sure you are listening to the points he or she is making.

7. Be patient: Recognize and accept that, with limited meeting time, not all comments or questions can be dealt with right away. Be willing to let some things go by. Pick your issues by choosing what is most important. Over time it is likely that the really important things will get discussed and dealt with.

8. Tolerate tension in yourself and in the group: Honest communication on difficult issues will inevitably lead to feeling uncomfortable, angry, or afraid during some parts of the meeting. There may also be times when people are arguing over their differences. A constructive family meeting allows for this, up to a point, as long as the conflict is bringing out unresolved issues and remaining respectful. The role of the leadership is to monitor how this is going and to lead it to some resolution. Rather than try to smooth things over just to avoid conflict, tolerate feeling uncomfortable as best as you can.

In disciplined and productive family meetings focused on teamwork, participants accept that the group is as important as the individual. When individuals do what is supportive of the meeting, the meeting can take care of the needs of each individual. Put the group's interests first and you will be more likely to get what you need.

Notes

CHAPTER ONE

1. All case examples and anecdotes are either amalgamations of actual situations, alterations of client cases with identifying information removed or changed, or illustrations to make a point.

2. US Trust. Survey of Affluent Americans XXVI, 2007.

3. PNC Wealth Management. Wealth and Values Survey: Earned Wealth vs. Inherited Wealth, 2008.

4. PNC Wealth Management. Wealth and Values Survey: Millionaires and Legacy, 2012.

5. Jude Miller Burke and Mark Attridge, "Pathways to Career and Leadership Success: Part 1—A Psychosocial Profile of $100K Professionals," *Journal of Workplace Behavioral Health* 26 (2011): 207–239.

6. S.M. Miller. "Born on Third Base: Sources of Wealth of the 1997 Forbes 400," *United for a Fair Economy* (1997) http://www.faireconomy.org/press_room/1997/born_on_third_base_sources_of_wealth_of_1997_forbes_400.

7. "Born on Third Base: What the Forbes 400 Really Says about the Economic Equality and Opportunity in America," ed. Shannon Moriarty, *United for a Fair Economy* (2012) http://faireconomy.org/bornonthirdbase2012; Peter Bernstein, *All the Money in the World: How the Forbes 400 Make—and Spend—Their Fortunes*. (USA: First Vintage Books, 2007).

8. Billionaire fortunes tend to have a moderately higher proportion of multigenerational wealth due to several reasons: the time it takes to build the wealth, the fact that multigenerational family businesses constitute a larger portion of significant wealth, and the reality that these fortunes are more typical of mature economies which support the development and maintenance of large fortunes. In today's emerging economies where great entrepreneurial expansion is occurring, around 16 percent–18 percent of fortunes come from inheritance alone or inheritance plus growth of business and investment. See Forbes Insights: *Global Wealth and Family Ties, 2012*, and Ledbury Research/Barclays Wealth—Barclays Wealth Insights Volume 14: *The Transfer of Trust:Wealth and Succession in a Changing World, 2011*.

9. Data derived from US Census Bureau and private surveys such as the annual Capgemini/RBC World Wealth Reports (previously Capgemini/Merrill Lynch World Wealth Report).

10. *The Oxford Dictionary of Proverbs* comments that this phrase is often attributed to Andrew Carnegie but it is not found in any of his published writings. It is possible Carnegie, a Scot, was simply reworking the Irish/Scottish proverb

"there's nothing but three generations between a clog and a clog" and was quoted in doing so.

11. Most analyses of wealth focus on the macro level, i.e., the socioeconomic impact of class qualities or inequalities on a societal level. They try to articulate the influence of power and privilege for society as a whole or to the identities of wealth's constituents. Cultural aspects are intertwined with elements such as rank, value, or power. For greater discussion of the role of power in transforming the core of culture into the complexities of class, see Heather E. Bullock and Wendy M. Limbert, "Class," in *Critical Psychology: An Introduction, 2nd Edition,* eds. Dennis R. Fox, Isaac Prilletensky, and Stephanie Austin (London, England: Sage Publications, 2009), 215–231. Although class and power are indeed critical lenses through which to view wealth's impact, socioeconomic discussions of wealth may not illuminate very well what happens at the individual and intra-familial level. To grasp the personal experience of individual and family wealth, specifically regarding the process of adaptation within and across generations, the analysis of wealth as culture provides a fresh perspective.

CHAPTER TWO

12. Drawn from my professional experience and the groundbreaking book by Amy Domini, Dennis Pearne, and Sharon Rich, *The Challenges of Wealth: Mastering the Personal and Financial Conflicts* (Dow Jones-Irwin, 1988).

13. This and many of the subsequent data on US economic demographics are derived from analyses of the Federal Reserve: *Survey of Consumer Finances (SCF), 2010* and prior SCFs, and secondary sources such as *The Wall Street Journal* analyses of SCF data. As of the end of 2012, a net worth of $1 million qualified as being at approximately the 92nd percentile of US households.

14. US Federal Reserve Board. *Survey of Consumer Finances, 2012.*

15. The personal savings rate of the US population used to vary between approximately 7.5 percent and 12.5 percent prior to the 1990s (US Department of Commerce: *Bureau of Economic Analysis*) but steadily dropped toward zero between 2005 and 2007 until rebounding in recent years to around 3–5 percent. This figure, however, is highly skewed between the 39 percent of US households who save portions of their income on a regular basis (US Federal Reserve: *Survey of Consumer Finances 2012*) and the majority of US households who do not. Compare this personal savings rate to that of Europe (typically over 20 percent) or the high-savings-rate countries of Japan and China (typically 35–40 percent).

16. Laura Saunders, "Baby You're a Rich Man," *The Wall Street Journal,* December 29, 2012. US Federal Reserve Board and Tax Policy Center, 2012.

17. US Federal Reserve Board. *Survey of Consumer Finances, 2012.*

18. US Federal Reserve Board. *Survey of Consumer Finances, 2012.*

19. Edward Iwata: "$1 million: Now that we have your attention, what's the infatuation with that number?" *USA Today,* August 15, 2006.

20. Fidelity Investments: *Fidelity Millionaire Outlook study, 2012.*

21. Capgemini/RBC Wealth Management: *World Wealth Report 2013.* Note that published figures by The Spectrem Group, an affluent-marketing and industry survey organization that also studies the wealthy, point to more than double the figures of Capgemini/RBC and others. In 2012, the Spectrem Group announced that number of US households with investable net worth was 8.6 million. They also reported figures of 1.078 million with at least $5 million and 107,000 households with greater than $25 million.

22. US Census Bureau: *American Community Survey, 2011.*

23. "Forbes 400," *Forbes,* 2012.

CHAPTER THREE

24. In Canada and in some other countries, the term "natives" specifically denotes indigenous peoples originally occupying the land. For those readers I offer the term "natural-born citizens" when referring to those born and raised in the Land of Wealth, as opposed to immigrants.

25. Readers confused by my including upper-middle-class culture as not necessarily part of wealth need to understand that wealth is relative. Certainly, anyone traveling from poverty to upper-middle-class will feel and be an Immigrant to wealth in that transition. What must be acknowledged is that people born in the upper-middle-class who later become much, much wealthier feel and are Immigrants in their own right. This seems incredulous to middle-class observers who consider the near-wealthy and the ultra-wealthy all part of the same group, differing only by a couple of zeros in net worth. This point will be mentioned briefly in an upcoming section on Immigrant-Native Hybrids in wealth.

26. Here and throughout this book I rely heavily on the many writings of John W. Berry, Ph.D., and other professionals in the field of cross-cultural psychology. For an overview of the research and thinking in this area, see resources such as David L. Sam and John W. Berry, (eds.), *The Cambridge Handbook of Acculturation Psychology* (Cambridge: Cambridge University Press, 2006).

27. "Acculturation" is the broader, more inclusive term for adaptation strategies compared to "assimilation," the term more familiar to most people. Assimilation is only one method of acculturation among many.

28. *Born Rich,* directed by Jamie Johnson, (2003; HBO), Film.

29. See the website of the Family Firm Institute (http://www.ffi.org) for a review of statistics and the substantial body of research on family firms, their influence, and their generational patterns and stresses.

30. David Bork, "It Ain't Easy to Be Rich: Discovering Your Personal Net Worth," *Private Wealth,* 1997/98, 19–23.

31. Suniya S. Luthar, "The Culture of Affluence: Psychological Costs of Material Wealth," *Child Development,* 74, (2003): 1590.

32. Cynthia Garcia Coll and Amy Kerivan Marks (eds.), *The Immigrant Paradox in Children and Adolescents: Is Becoming American a Developmental Risk?* (Washington DC: American Psychological Association, 2012), 7, citing the work of Alejandro Portes and Ruben G. Rumbaut, *Immigrant America: A Portrait.* 3rd ed. (Berkeley: University of California Press, 2006), and others.

CHAPTER FOUR

33. John W. Berry, "Immigration, Acculturation and Adaptation," *Applied Psychology* 46, (1997): 5–68.

34. David L. Sam and John W. Berry, "Acculturation: When Individuals and Groups of Different Cultural Backgrounds Meet," *Perspectives on Psychological Science* 5, (2010): 472–481.

35. Dennis T. Jaffe and James A. Grubman, "Acquirers' and Inheritors' Dilemma: Finding Life Purpose and Building Personal Identity in the Presence of Wealth," *Journal of Wealth Management*, (Fall, 2007): 1–26.

36. David Brooks, *Bobos in Paradise* (New York, NY: Simon Schuster, 2001).

37. Robert Frank, *Richistan: A Journey Through the American Wealth Boom and the Lives of the New Rich* (New York, NY: Three Rivers Press, 2008); *The High-Beta Rich: How the Manic Wealthy Will Take Us To The Next Boom, Bubble, and Bust* (New York, NY: Crown Publishing Group, 2011).

38. Most of our knowledge of the wealth population comes from the wealth management industry or firms that market to the affluent or their advisors, rather than from well-researched studies in sociology or psychology. This is a sad commentary on the fields of psychology and sociology, including their biases against the wealthy as subjects for study and the many practical limitations that exist in research methodology and access to the wealthy. Detailed research exists from marketing firms such as the Spectrem Group, TNS, HNW, Capgemini, and Russ Prince and Associates. These industry studies, of varying degrees of quality in research design and analysis, provide most of what we know about the wealthy.

39. Russ Alan Prince, "Nine High Net Worth Personalities," *On Wall Street*, (October 1997) 2–3. See also: Phoenix Wealth Management/Harris Interactive *Wealth Survey, 2003*. Subtypes in the Phoenix study included Deal Masters, Altruistic Achievers, Secret Succeeders, Status Chasers, Satisfied Savers, and Disengaged Inheritors. Of interest is that the Disengaged Inheritors subgroup comprised 13 percent of the survey respondents while the other subgroups were predominantly acquirers of wealth, in line with the expected proportion of Immigrants versus Natives.

40. Hannah Shaw Grove and Russ Alan Prince, "Understanding the Wealthy," *The Psychology of Wealth* 1, No. 1 (2008).

41. See research-derived clusters of money personalities determined by Dr. Kathleen Gurney and her colleagues at http://www.financialpsychology.com and by Hugh Massie and colleagues at http://www.financialdna.com.

42. John W. Berry, "Contexts of Acculturation," in David L. Sam and John W. Berry (eds), *The Cambridge Handbook of Acculturation Psychology* (Cambridge: Cambridge University Press, 2006): 27.

43. For a review of trends in demographics of wealth, see James Grubman, "Evolving Your Practice to Serve the Next Generation of High Net-Worth Families," *Pioneer Investments* (2010), later revised by Kathleen Burns Kingsbury.

44. Seth J. Schwartz, Jennifer B. Unger, Byron L. Zamboanga, and Jose Szapocznik, "Rethinking the Concept of Acculturation," *American Psychologist*, 65(4), (2010): 237-251; Sam and Berry (2010); Margaret Gibson, "Immigrant Adaptation and Patterns of Acculturation," *Human Development*, 44 (2001):19–23. The three strategies listed here are an adaptation of the conceptual schemes of Schwartz et al. (2010) and the acculturation profiles named by John W. Berry and his colleagues in their various writings. Hopefully future research will clarify the actual subgroups and strategies that do exist in the wealth population.

45. This strategy is termed Separation in the cross-cultural psychology literature. I have used the more natural-language term Avoidance here, which has some extra associations that need explanation but sidesteps the somewhat awkward and jargon-like wording of Separation.

46. Berry (2006).

47. Jose A. Del Pilar & Jocelynda O. Udasco, "Deculturation: Its Lack of Validity," *Cultural Diversity and Ethnic Minority Psychology*, 10 (2004):169–176.; Seth J. Schwartz & Byron L. Zamboanga, "Testing Berry's Model of Acculturation: A Confirmatory Latent Class Approach," *Cultural Diversity and Ethnic Minority Psychology*, 14 (2008): 275–285; Schwartz et al. (2010).

48. It would be important to distinguish between those who are choosing some degree of Avoidance compared to those who are being truly marginalized. I would encourage readers who have good examples of marginalized immigrants to wealth to contact me via email through my website at http://www .jamesgrubman.com.

49. This graphic is adapted with only minor changes from the models delineated by John W. Berry, as in his article, "Acculturation: Living Successfully in Two Cultures," *International Journal of Intercultural Relations*, 29 (2005): 697–712.

CHAPTER FIVE

50. *Driving Miss Daisy*, directed by Bruce Beresford, performed by Jessica Tandy, Morgan Freeman, Dan Ackroyd (1989; The Zanuck Company, Warner Brothers), Film.

51. Thomas Stanley and William Danko, *The Millionaire Next Door* (Lanham, MD: Taylor Trade Publishing, 1996/2010).

52. Christopher Mogil, Peter Woodrow, and Ann Slepian, *We Gave Away a Fortune: Stories of People Who Have Devoted Themselves and Their Wealth to Peace,*

Justice and a Healthy Environment (Gabriola Island, BC: New Society Publishers, 1991). Note that Chris Mogil and Anne Ellinger's current organization, Bolder Giving, helps sponsor the Billionaire Giving Pledge which encourages wealth's immigrants and natives to devote 50 percent or more of their wealth to philanthropy prior to or upon death. However, giving away 50 percent of wealth at the *Forbes 400* level (currently around $2 billion and above) still leaves $1 billion or more to future generations within the family. It is only at the level of giving away perhaps 80 percent–90 percent of personal wealth that a return to middle-class life is truly likely.

53. Associated Press, "Man's Will Leaves Hidden Wealth to Montana," *The New York Times*, November 13, 2005 or http://www.nytimes.com/2005/11/13/national/13montana.html.

54. Kelly Kearsley, "When Dad Secretly Amasses a Fortune," *The Wall Street Journal Wealth Management*, July 22, 2013.

55. This idea that the benchmark of normality is the middle class also grows from the demographic reality that the middle-class culture is the dominant, majority culture in American society. Wealth's immigrants from the middle-class have the luxury of assuming their background is the standard of comparison for any other culture to which they may travel.

56. For a fuller description of this crucial issue in wealthy families, see James Grubman, "Privacy Versus Secrecy," *More than Money Journal* (2001) available at http://www.morethanmoney.org or my website http://www.jamesgrubman.com.

57. In my experience, the estate planning attorney present for these meetings before or after the parents' demise often shares the perspective of the parents, not that of the next generation. Focused on delivering the glad tidings, the attorney is taken aback by what seems like the ingratitude of spoiled children. He or she is rarely sympathetic to the shock of the heirs about the secret, not the money. This can damage the ensuing relationship with the attorney, with especially dire consequences if the attorney is named trustee for the beneficiaries now sitting across from him.

CHAPTER SIX

58. *Wall Street*, directed by Oliver Stone, performed by Michael Douglas and Charlie Sheen, (1987; Twentieth Century Fox), Film.

59. *The Queen of Versailles,* directed by Lauren Greenfield, performed by David and Jackie Siegel, (2012; Magnolia Pictures), Film.

60. Frank, *Richistan*.

61. See James Grubman, Kathleen Bollerud and Cheryl Holland, "Helping the Overspending Client," *Journal of Financial Planning,* (March 2011): 60–67, as well as books such as April Benson, *To Buy or Not to Buy: Why We Overshop and How to Stop* (Boston, MA: Trumpeter Press, 2008). Interested readers should also investigate the excellent writings by professionals such as Bill Messinger,

Sam Dresser, Terry Hunt, Doug Lyons, James Olan Hutcheson, and others in the field of addiction and family business/family wealth.

62. This excellent axiom appears in many of Thayer Willis' writings, *Navigating the Dark Side of Wealth: A Life Guide for Inheritors* (Portland, OR: New Concord Press, 2003). See http://www.thayerwillis.com for further writings and her latest resource for inheritors, *Beyond Gold: True Wealth for Inheritors* (Portland, OR: New Concord Press, 2012).

CHAPTER SEVEN

63. Interested readers who come across examples of well-adjusted immigrants to wealth in literature or film should please email me through my website http://www.jamesgrubman.com.

64. John W. Berry, "Acculturation: Living Successfully in Two Cultures," *International Journal of Intercultural Relations* 29 (2005): 697-712.

65. Alfred Lubrano, *Limbo: Blue Collar Roots, White Collar Dreams* (Hoboken, New Jersey: John Wiley & Sons, Inc, 2005).

66. Lubrano, *Limbo,* 193–223.

67. Lubrano, *Limbo,* 194.

68. See summary of recent demographic research by Mary Quist Newins, accessed July 6, 2013, http://www.thewealthchannel.com/women-and-finance/articles/women-and-money.

69. If the psychosocial distance between cultures or the conflicts between the heritage and receiving cultures aren't too broad, Integration or biculturalism tends to be most possible and the least stressful of acculturation strategies. See reviews in Schwartz et al. (2010) and Sam and Berry (2006) as well as the article by Veronica Benet-Martinez and Jana Haritatos, "Bicultural Identity Integration: Components and Psychosocial Antecedents." *Journal of Personality* 73:4 (2005): 1015–1050.

70. This phenomenon, known as the acculturation gap, can surface in especially difficult ways between parents and children adjusting to a new culture. See this discussion later in this chapter.

71. Interested readers should investigate the NEO-PI-R personality inventory and associated research on the dimension of Openness in parenting.

72. See the excellent analysis of the complexities of acculturation gaps in the review by Eva H. Telzer, "Expanding the Acculturation Gap-Distress Model: An Integrative Review of Research," *Human Development* 53 (2010): 313-340.

73. Suniya S. Luthar, "The Culture of Affluence: Psychological Costs of Material Wealth," *Child Development* 74(6) (2003): 1581–1593; Suniya S. Luthar and Samuel H. Barkin, "Are Affluent Youth Truly 'At Risk'? Vulnerability and Resilience Across Three Diverse Samples," *Development and Psychopathology* 24 (2012): 429–449; Suniya S. Luthar and Shawn J. Latendresse, "Children of the Affluent: Challenges to Well-Being," *Current Directions in Psychological Science* 14(1) (2005):49–53.

74. Nadia S. Ansary and Suniya S. Luthar, "Distress and Academic Achievement Among Adolescents of Affluence: A Study of Externalizing and Internalizing Problem Behaviors and School Performance," *Development and Psychopathology* 21 (2009): 319–341; Suniya S. Luthar, Karen A. Shoum, and Pamela J. Brown, "Extracurricular Involvement Among Affluent Youth: A Scapegoat for 'Ubiquitous Achievement Pressures'?" *Developmental Psychology* 42 (2006): 583–597.

75. See research by the Center for Wealth and Philanthropy at Boston College and the Center on Philanthropy at Indiana University for excellent summaries on charitable giving, wealth, and inheritance.

CHAPTER EIGHT

76. Very recent research on successful multigenerational global families is bearing this out. Dennis T. Jaffe, "Good Fortune: Building a Hundred Year Family Enterprise," (Wise Counsel Research, 2013) Available at http:// wisecounselresearch.com or http://dennisjaffe.com.

77. For more detail on the fundamental financial skills needed for a successful adult life, see the writings about the Financial Skills Trust, as in the article by Jon Gallo, Eileen Gallo, and James Grubman, "Not Your Typical Incentive Trust: The ROTE and FST, Part II," *Journal of Financial Planning* (April 2011): 36–39; as well as books by Jon Gallo and Eileen Gallo, Joline Godfrey, Jayne Pearl and Richard Morris, and many others.

78. Readers familiar with the law will note I use the word "capacity" here in a manner similar to legal terminology. Having a capacity such as testamentary capacity, mental capacity for medical decision-making, or financial capacity for managing ones' own affairs subsumes a variety of component skills needed for that capacity. The component skills for a capacity for independence, for example, include much more than just financial literacy. I believe a robust capacity for independence requires a broad range of skills that help an individual survive through good times and bad.

79. Readings for inheritors include Jessie O'Neill's *The Golden Ghetto: The Psychology of Affluence* (The Affluenza Project, 1997) also Thayer Willis' two books, *Navigating the Dark Side of Wealth* and *Beyond Gold*; Myra Salzer's *The Inheritor's Sherpa: A Life-Summiting Guide for Inheritors* (Portland, OR: New Concord Press, 2005) and *Living Richly: Seizing the Potential of Inherited Wealth* (Boulder, CO: Legacy Publishing, LLC, 2010). Other excellent resources by and for inheritors are available from The Inheritance Project at http://www .inheritance-project.com.

80. Readers should understand that many therapists are not well trained in handling the unique issues and life experiences of the wealthy. Many therapists don't understand how wealth truly is a culture of its own, so these therapists extrapolate from their standard training and their middle-class perspectives. I would encourage readers seeking psychological help for wealth issues to contact the Financial Therapy Association at http://www.financialtherapyassociation

.com or to use search terms on the Internet such as wealth counseling, psychology and wealth, wealth psychology, and the like.

81. A good place to locate high-quality resources is the Resource page of The Redwoods Initiative at http://www.redwoodsinitiative.com.

82. Dennis T. Jaffe "From Child to Citizen of the Family Enterprise: The Five Act Family Drama of Next Generation Development," *Journal of Practical Estate Planning* (December–January 2010), 49–58.

CHAPTER NINE

83. See discussions of the strong family focus of blue-collar and working-class life in Lubrano's *Limbo*, and the excellent overview of generational poverty by Ruby Payne, *A Framework for Understanding Poverty* (Highlands, TX: aha! Process, 2005).

84. Proponents of family systems thinking will understand this model as balancing the important elements of family cohesion with personal individuation. Too much cohesion and not enough individuation lead to dependency, enmeshment, and dysfunctional boundaries, all of which are evident in dysfunctional families of wealth. Too much individuation fails to grow shared decision-making, collective identity, and familial bonds, leading to splintering of the family wealth. Balancing cohesion and individuation is hard when wealth enters the picture. Yet families who accomplish this succeed best across generations.

85. I am indebted to Malcolm Gladwell who first mentioned the immigrant paradox to me during our discussions about the Immigrant/Native metaphor of the wealthy.

86. Coll and Marks, Eds., *The Immigrant Paradox* (2011), 4.

87. Coll and Marks, Eds., *The Immigrant Paradox* (2011).

CHAPTER TEN

88. Pierre Bourdieau, "The Forms of Capital," *Handbook of Theory and Research for the Sociology of Education,* ed. J. Richardson, trans. H. Nice (New York, Greenwood 2007), 241–258.

89. The groundbreaking contributions of Jay Hughes, Dennis Jaffe, Kelin Gersick, Ivan Lansberg, Lee Hausner, and many others are acknowledged here. Although different colleagues have talked variously about four, five, or six capitals of the family, I have found it easiest to condense these to the four capitals described in this section.

90. See the excellent book on family wealth by Lee Hausner, *Children of Paradise: Successful Parenting for Prosperous Families* (Los Angeles, CA: Tarcher Press, 1990); Lee Hausner and Douglas Freeman, *The Legacy Family: The Definitive Guide to Creating a Successful Multigenerational Family* (New York, NY: Palgrave Macmillan, 2009); and Lee Hausner and Ernest Doud Jr., *Hats Off to You 2: Balancing Roles and Creating Success in Family Business* (2004).

91. Dennis T. Jaffe, *Stewardship in Your Family Enterprise* (Pioneer Imprints: 2009).

92. Willis, *Navigating the Dark Side of Wealth* (2003).

93. Two notable programs are those run by The Redwoods Initiative, based on the East Coast, and Independent Means, based on the West Coast.

94. Adapted from an article written by James Grubman, "Of Treasured Kids and Treasure Hunts" *Pitcairn Family Newsletter* (Winter, 2011) which was inspired by an example described in an article by Eileen Gallo, "Helping Grandparents Model Good Behaviors," *Journal of Financial Planning* (October, 2010): 44–47.

95. James E. Hughes, Jr., *Family Wealth: Keeping It in the Family, Revised Edition* (Princeton NJ: Bloomberg Press; 2004).

96. Jaffe, "Good Fortune." 2013.

APPENDIX I

97. Alexis de Tocqueville. *Democracy in America,* edited by J.P. Mayer, translated by George Lawrence (London, UK: Saunders and Otley, 1850, reprint 1966), 635.

98. Stanley Lebergott, *The American Economy: Income, Wealth, and Want.* (Princeton, NJ: Princeton University Press, 1976), 172.

About the Author

JAMES GRUBMAN PH.D. is a senior psychologist and consultant to families of wealth, their advisors, and prominent resources in the financial services industry. He works with ultra-high-net-worth families on issues such as financial education, succession planning, estate planning, and family communication. He also provides consultation and training to family offices and wealth advisory firms about client relationship skills, family dynamics, and organizational issues in wealth management.

As a faculty member at Bentley University, Dr. Grubman created the first graduate-level-only course in the United States on the psychology of financial planning. He has also helped design and teach the family-dynamics topic area for the Certified Private Wealth Advisor certificate sponsored by the Investment Management Consultants Association (IMCA) and the University of Chicago Booth School of Business. He has presented for such organizations as the Family Firm Institute, the National Association of Personal Financial Advisors, the Institute for Private Investors, TIGER 21, the Heckerling Institute, and the Family Office Association, among many others. He has written multiple articles in publications such as the *Journal of Wealth Management,* the *Journal of Financial Planning,* and *Private Wealth* magazine. A member of the Boston Estate Planning Council and the Society of Trust and Estate Practitioners, Dr. Grubman has earned the Family Business Advising certificate from the Family Firm Institute. He maintains a specialty interest as a neuropsychologist in the issue of how ADHD and learning disorders impact entrepreneurs and their families. For more information, see www.JamesGrubman.com.

Made in the USA
Lexington, KY
06 October 2014